HOPKINSON HOUSE.

KANGCHENJUNGA
THE UNTRODDEN PEAK

The way up to the Hump

KANGCHENJUNGA
THE UNTRODDEN PEAK

Charles Evans

LONDON
HODDER & STOUGHTON

First printed 1956

PRINTED AND BOUND IN ENGLAND FOR
HODDER AND STOUGHTON LTD., BY
HAZELL WATSON AND VINEY LTD., AYLESBURY AND LONDON

To The

Members of the Expedition

ACKNOWLEDGEMENTS

SOME of those who in various ways generously helped the expedition I have named in the book. Of others, I should like in particular to thank here the following: Mr. Stuart Bain; Mr. T. D. Bourdillon; Mr. H. Bradley; Mr. and Mrs. C. Briggs; Dr. John Cotes; Mr. David Fisher; Major G. K. Franklin of the War Office; Mrs. Goodfellow; Mr. H. Grimwade of the British Boot, Shoe and Allied Trades Research Association; the late Mr. A. P. Hartley; Mr. R. S. Horsman; Dr. Thelwall Jones; Dr. Arthur Kelly; Mr. D. Lacy-Hulbert; Mr. Eric Mensforth; Dr. D. R. Seaton; Mr. C. J. Sharkey; Mr. S. H. Staff; Mr. Bradford Washburn; Sir Harold Whittingham; the permanent staff of the Royal Geographical Society; the staff of The Chesterfield Tube Co., Ltd.; Mr. F. Lewin Harris and the staff of The British Oxygen Co., Ltd.; Mr. E. H. Wheeldon and the staff of Messrs. Normalair, Ltd.; the many firms who gave or lent us stores and equipment gratis or at much reduced prices; the staff of Messrs. Mackinnon, Mackenzie, Ltd., Bombay; Mr. B. P. Robinson and the staff of the Anchor Line, Ltd.; the officials of H.M. Customs and Excise who were concerned with our baggage; the Indian Ministry of External Affairs; Mr. Paul Buxton, of the U.K. High Commission in India; Colonel R. R. Proud, of the British Embassy in Nepal; the local secretaries of the Himalayan Club, Mr. A. R. Leyden in Bombay, Mr. T. H. Braham in Calcutta, and Mr. R. Hotz in Delhi; All-India Radio, the B.B.C., and Mr. B. N. Sreenivasaiah, of the Meteorological Office, New Delhi, for weather forecasts; and the Indian Air Force for the splendid photographs they gave us of the mountain.

On my own behalf, I thank Sir Edwin Herbert, then President of the Alpine Club, for the club's invitation to me to lead the expedition; the President and Council of the Royal Geographical Society for their ready agreement to join in sponsoring it; and Sir John Hunt, chairman of the Kangchenjunga committee, for his support, and particularly for the suggestion that led to my having the help of Mr. A. W. Bridge.

Finally, I wish to acknowledge the help that I have had in the writing of this book, and to thank the members of the expedition for lending me their diaries, answering questions, and reading the story. Mr. Michael Davis, of Messrs. Hodder and Stoughton, Ltd., helped me to check many of the facts, and to assemble the maps and illustrations. The title was suggested by Mr. Kenneth Tarbuck.

To Mr. Douglas Milner I am especially grateful, for his kindness in undertaking to prepare the photographs, and for the care and great skill with which he has done so.

CHARLES EVANS

July 1956

CONTENTS

APPENDICES

COLOUR PLATES

MONOCHROME PLATES

xiii

MONOCHROME PLATES

MAPS

DIAGRAMS

FOREWORD

By His Royal Highness the Duke of Edinburgh, K.G.

This is the story of how Kangchenjunga was climbed. It was a brilliant achievement in terms of planning, organisation and execution. It was also much more than that: it was from start to finish a great adventure by a band of enthusiasts. With the support of their hardy and skilful Sherpa companions, they tackled and overcame one of the most difficult problems in the Himalayas and, quite evidently, enjoyed almost every minute of it.

Patron, Kangchenjunga Expedition, 1955.

xix

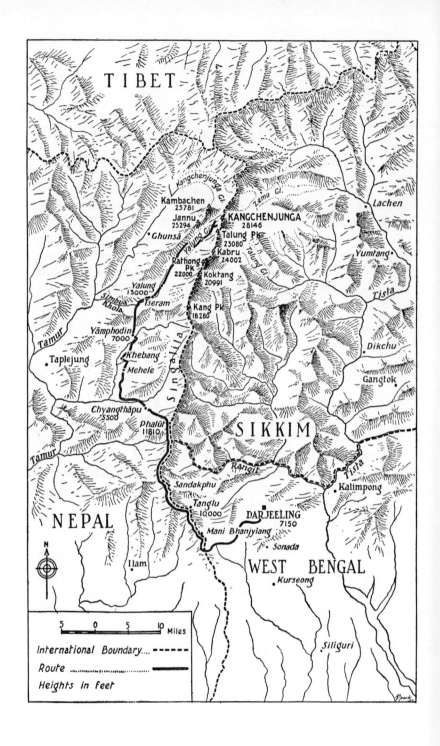

CHAPTER ONE

INTRODUCTION

NORTH of Darjeeling the ridge on which the town stands drops steeply for six thousand feet. On its west flank is Rungneet bungalow. From the lawn the terraced gardens fall towards the distant Rangit river, and the eye, bridging the gulf of the valley, sees in the blue haze crest beyond crest of jungle-clad foothills rising towards the snows. There, forty-six miles away, is Kangchenjunga. Brilliant in sunshine, cold in shadow, it seems to float above the darkness of the valleys and the lower ranges, filling the north-western horizon.

Kangchenjunga is the centre and highest point of a spur of the main Himalayan chain, which here, eighty miles to the east of Everest, is not well defined. The spur juts to the south, over-looking the plains of India. It is shaped like a cross, each of its arms a range of high mountains. The northern arm stretches to the Tibetan frontier thirteen miles away; its summits are the Twins, Nepal Peak, Tent Peak, Pyramid Peak, Langpo Peak, Langpo Chung and Domo. The southern arm leads to the north end of the Singalila ridge, twenty miles away; its summits are Kangchenjunga II, Talung Peak, Kabru, Ratong Peak, Koktang and Kang Peak. The western arm includes the unnamed west peak of Kangchenjunga, Kambachen, and Jannu. The eastern arm runs from Kangchenjunga II to the Zemu gap, and on to Simvu and Siniolchu in Sikkim. In the four quadrants enclosed by these ridges are four glaciers: in the north-east the Zemu glacier, seventeen miles long; in the south-east the Talung glacier, eight miles long; in the north-west the Kangchenjunga glacier, eleven

I

miles long; and in the south-west the Yalung glacier, thirteen miles long. The Zemu and Talung glaciers drain into the Tista river; the Kangchenjunga and Yalung drain into the Tamur river, the Yalung by way of the Simbua Khola. The north and south arms of the cross, with their southward continuation, the Singalila ridge, form the watershed between the rivers of Nepal and of Sikkim. The whole west face of Kangchenjunga lies in Nepal, the whole east face in Sikkim.

From Mani Bhanjyiang, by Darjeeling, the Singalila ridge runs west a short way, then north as far as Kang Peak, and it stays high. At Phalut, only three days from Darjeeling, it is twelve thousand feet above the sea. A short way north of Phalut, the ridge divides Nepal from Sikkim; south of Phalut it divides Nepal from Bengal. It is a beautiful trekking route; a pony track runs through rhododendron forest along its crest; from it are seen the great peaks grouped around Everest, and, close at hand, the mass of Kangchenjunga. It is one of the highways from Darjeeling into eastern Nepal.

The first European to describe the country around Kangchenjunga was Sir Joseph Hooker: in 1848 and 1849 he visited the valleys on every side of it, and his book, *Himalayan Journals*, is full of careful observation and lively description. Many later travellers, both European and Asian, explored the neighbourhood; but though the idea of climbing the mountain was suggested as early as 1882, no attempt to do so was made until 1905. The first climber to study it closely with a view to finding a way up it was Douglas Freshfield, who in 1899 made a circuit of it. He suggested that there might be a route on the Yalung face, writing in the *Alpine Journal*: " . . . the rockwall at the head of the Yalung glacier might be overcome by the help of a shelf conspicuous to the right of a horseshoe cliff. . . . The western ridge would be gained close to the foot of the final peak and not far below it."

Six years later this route was tried. A party under the leadership of Aleister Crowley visited the Yalung; they met with an avalanche accident, and four men were killed, Lieutenant Pache and three porters. Pache was buried at the foot of the slope on a moraine hillock, now called Pache's Grave.

The Yalung was then unvisited until 1920, when Raeburn, one of the most experienced mountaineers of his time, went there with C. G. Crawford. Once again the likely route was noted by an experienced eye, and Raeburn, in Vol. XXXIV of the *Alpine Journal*, wrote: "Our aim was to gain a white mantle of snow which from Darjeeling may be seen to lie across the broad bosom of Kangchen, with a sickle-shaped gorget of rock at its upper extremity." But the party was small and lightly equipped, and could not make a serious attempt on the face. Freshfield's shelf and Raeburn's white mantle of snow are now known as the Great Shelf, and Freshfield's horseshoe cliff and Raeburn's sickle-shaped gorget of rock are known as the Sickle.

For thirty years, except for the visit of a solitary American, Edgar Francis Farmer, who disappeared on the upper reaches of the Yalung glacier, no climber came again to this valley. Those were the years of the three expeditions to Kangchenjunga, of Bauer in 1929 and 1931, and of Dyhrenfurth in 1930. The tale of the exploits of Bauer's party on the north-east spur of the mountain above the Zemu glacier, of their struggle up it for weeks on end, and of their equally laborious struggle down it in bad weather, greatly stirred the climbing world. On their second expedition, after surmounting all the difficulties of the spur they turned back from 25,263 feet rather than embark on a snow-slope which they saw to be dangerous. Their effort was a classical example of skill, courage, energy and judgement. Dyhrenfurth's huge expedition of 1930, to the north-west face of the mountain, was described by F. S. Smythe, who was a member of the expedition, in his book, *The Kangchenjunga Adventure*. So far, every visit to the moun-

3

tain had been either at the end of the monsoon, or during it: Crowley had met with disaster on September 1st, and Raeburn and Crawford had been in the Yalung in late September; Bauer's first expedition had done most of its climbing during September, and his second expedition during July and August. Dyhrenfurth arrived at the foot of the mountain in the last week of April, and so was the first to be in the right place at what we now regard as the right time, the month of May. Towards mid-May there is a regular change in the pattern of the weather in the mountains of eastern Nepal: the north-westerly winds prevalent in the first half of the year slacken, and there is a short and variable, but fairly dependable, spell of fine still weather before the onset of the south-west monsoon at the beginning of June, the monsoon that brings not only heavy snowfall on the higher slopes, but warmth, which rots the deep snow through and through and makes it dangerous.

Dyhrenfurth came, it is true, at the right time, but unfortunately he went to a face of the mountain more menaced than any other by ice-cliffs, and the expedition turned away from Kangchenjunga after the loss of the Sherpa Chettan in an avalanche, and the failure of the party to find an alternative route. The highest point reached was about 21,000 feet.

In those years, while the Yalung face was neglected, the reputation of Kangchenjunga for bad weather and dangerous ice-avalanche grew: the mountain came to be regarded as more subject to ice-avalanche than any other, and more exposed to heavy snowfall. Smythe, in his widely read book, condemned the Yalung face on the ground that, as a south face, it would be unusually subject to the danger of avalanche, a view not now held to be supported by experience; he thought that the Great Shelf seen from Darjeeling would itself be menaced by avalanche.

This gives the measure of the credit due to Lewis and

4

1 Kangchenjunga from Rungneet

George Band

Joe Brown

John Clegg

Charles Evans

Norman Hardie

John Jackson

Tom MacKinnon

Annullu

Neil Mather

Dawa Tenzing

Tony Streather

Urkien

Da Tsering

Changjup

Lobsang

Topke

Pasang Sonar

Ang Temba

Kempe, who, in the face of established opinion, came to believe that a route might be found here.

In 1951 Gilmour Lewis and the late George Frey visited the Yalung, a visit which resulted directly in Lewis's return there two years later with John Kempe. From the slopes of Kabru in 1953 Kempe studied Kangchenjunga and concluded that there was indeed a chance worth exploring on the Yalung face. In describing this expedition Kempe wrote very cautiously: "an ascent does not seem out of the question from this side. We had no binoculars and it would not be safe to pass judgement on the final rock ridge running to the summit, but the general slope is not steep. Since at the time of writing Sikkim is barred this may be the only way to climb the mountain."

While Kempe studied the upper part of the Yalung face from Kabru, Lewis visited the upper part of the Yalung glacier to examine the lower part of the face; he concluded that here there were three possible lines worth investigation, and in 1954 a further expedition was organized by these two.

They asked Trevor Braham, secretary of the Himalayan Club, Ron Jackson, John Tucker and Dr. Stafford Matthews to join them, and in April 1954 they were back again in the Yalung.

The most conspicuous feature of the Yalung face is 'the Great Shelf', a hanging glacier lying on the face at between 23,500 feet and 25,500 feet. It is nearly a mile long by a quarter of a mile wide, and its long axis lies roughly north-west and south-east. Towards the north-west it slopes upwards, as it does also towards the north-east, its inner edge being several hundred feet higher than its outer.

North and east of the Shelf, the cliffs above it are steep and smooth; but north-west, to the east of the conspicuous cirque which Raeburn called the Gorget, and we the Sickle, is a steep snow-covered incline leading towards a point on the ridge

5

between Kangchenjunga and Kangchenjunga West; this incline we called the Gangway.

At the outer edge of the Shelf, for the southerly two-thirds of its length, is a five-thousand-foot cliff, falling to the head of the Yalung, and swept by avalanches of ice. At the south-eastern end of the Shelf a ridge of snow and ice, the Hogsback, runs south-west from the south ridge of Kangchenjunga II to end abruptly as the Great Buttress, which is the southerly boundary of the cliffs below the Great Shelf. South of the Hogsback and the Great Buttress is the Talung Cwm, a glacial cirque below Talung Saddle; south of that again is Talung Peak. The northern part of the outer edge of the Great Shelf does not break away abruptly: the ice flows gradually over it westwards, to form a steep glacier face, the Upper Icefall. North of the Upper Icefall is a depression, the Valley, overhung by ice-cliffs at the edge of the northernmost part of the Shelf. The north or right bank of the Valley is the south face of Kangchenjunga West.

The Upper Icefall flows west, falling three thousand feet at an angle which varies little, and which must be about forty-five degrees. Then at 20,500 feet the ice turns sharply south, and forms a level ice-field, the Plateau, half a mile long and a quarter of a mile wide. At its south end, the ice of the Plateau divides into two streams, east and west. Between them is a rock buttress, its top at 19,500 feet, called Kempe's Buttress. To the east of it the ice falls down gullies between Kempe's Buttress and the rock face below the southern part of the Great Shelf; to the west of it is the Lower Icefall, which at 18,000 feet reaches the valley floor.

Kempe's Buttress forms the left bank of the Lower Icefall. Its right, west, bank is formed by a prominent ridge which falls southwards from the west ridge of Kangchenjunga West. This is at first merely a low ridge in an ice-face; as it descends it becomes more prominent, standing out from the face in one

6

The Yalung face from Corner Camp

place as the horizontal ridge of snow and ice which we called the Hump. This part of it bounds the Plateau on the west. Its lowest part, the Western Buttress, is bold and rocky: towards the east, towards the Lower Icefall, it is sheer; towards the west it is less steep; here are slopes of snow, broken in places by bands of ice-cliffs. These are the slopes above Pache's Grave, and it was probably on these slopes that the accident happened to Crowley's party.

This is the face that Lewis and Kempe returned to explore in 1954. Like Freshfield and Raeburn, they thought that the key to the mountain was the Great Shelf. To it there were two likely ways: either by the Plateau and Upper Icefall, or by the Talung Cwm and over the Hogsback. Should these ways to the Great Shelf prove to be impassable, there was still a chance of a way to the top by the slopes above Pache's Grave; this route, it was thought, would lead not to the Great Shelf, but to the west ridge of Kangchenjunga West, which would then have to be traversed in order to reach the main summit.

The expedition succeeded in reaching the Talung Cwm, but were of the opinion that the route to it was, as Raeburn had thought, dangerous, and that there was little chance from the Cwm of climbing over the Hogsback to the Great Shelf. About the Icefall and Plateau route they were more optimistic: they succeeded in climbing the lower part of the Lower Icefall both near its right bank and near its left bank; moreover, Jackson and Lewis found a good safe route up Kempe's Buttress, by which the lower part of the icefall could be altogether avoided. They thought that a route might be forced from the top of the buttress to the Plateau, and that above the Plateau the Upper Icefall might be avoided by going up the Valley under Kangchenjunga West.

During the expedition, some of its members had been in close touch with Sir John Hunt, and when they returned they sent reports to him. Sir John's interest in Kangchenjunga had long been keen: he had visited it in 1937 with C. R. Cooke, when Cooke discovered a way to its north col. The reports impressed him favourably, and at his recommendation the Alpine Club decided to launch a larger expedition, which the Royal Geographical Society was invited to join in sponsoring. A committee was formed of which Sir John was asked to be chairman. The Government of Nepal gave leave for the expedition, and H.R.H. The Duke of Edinburgh graciously consented to be its patron.

CHAPTER TWO

PREPARATION

M Y impression after studying the report of Kempe's party was that the lower part of the Yalung face was very formidable. The route by way of the Talung Cwm was too dangerous, and the fact that the slopes above Pache's Grave seemed to lead only to the traverse of Kangchenjunga West put them out of court as a way to the main peak. The only beginning that seemed at all promising was the route found by Ron Jackson up Kempe's Buttress, though it was a chance whether or not the icefall above it could in any particular year be forced, and clear also that any route there would be to some degree dangerous, and subject to change as the ice moved. I planned, therefore, to start up Kempe's Buttress, and explore the part of the Lower Icefall above it. If we reached the Plateau, it looked as if there would then be no place of comparable difficulty until we were above the Great Shelf; to win through to the Shelf and then to find our resources too small to let us attempt the final ridge would be to waste an opportunity that might not come again; and our preparations were therefore made on the assumption that our goal was the summit.

In August 1954, A. W. Bridge and I met to discuss plans. Himself a climber, he agreed to look after the secretarial work of the expedition. We settled on a sailing date that would let us reach Darjeeling by the second week of March, and be in the Yalung before the end of the month. There would be eight Europeans, or at most nine, in the party, and twenty-eight permanent Sherpas, twelve of them equipped to go very high, and the rest equipped for carrying to about 20,000 feet. For carrying to the Yalung we should have to rely on Darjeeling men, and for work below our base camp we hoped to have a variable number of Sherpa coolies and local men casually employed.

We listed what we should need, and Alf Bridge went ahead to see that we got it. This was but a small part of his work for the expedition; he belonged to it, and shared our plans and our hopes; on the mountain, indeed, it was often as though he were there himself.

Equipment for high-altitude climbing is now very nearly standardized: ours differed little from that used on Everest and on the 1954 New Zealand expedition to the Barun valley. Our oxygen apparatus was, however, of a better pattern than that of 1953. For the highest climbs I proposed to use only the simple and reliable open-circuit apparatus; and our cylinders were lighter and of greater capacity than any designed before.

While Alf Bridge was collecting equipment, I was collecting the party. There were, besides myself, eight: Norman Hardie, Tom MacKinnon, John Jackson, Neil Mather, Tony Streather, George Band, Joe Brown, and our doctor, John Clegg.

The oldest, and the biggest, was MacKinnon: he was forty-two, is over six foot, and at the beginning of the expedition weighed fourteen stone. The youngest, and the smallest, was Joe Brown: he was twenty-four, and is five foot six. The rest of us, both in age and in size, came between. We were in our thirties or late twenties.

Our experience had much in common, though there were some unusual variations. Mather, unlike many first-rate climbers, had a fondness for fell-walks of fifty, sixty, or seventy miles at a stretch. He, Brown and Clegg were the only three who had not been to the Himalayas. Streather, on the other hand, had only once been to the Alps; he had served with the army of Pakistan, where he had confined himself to mountains of over 25,000 feet; on these he had twice been to more than that height. Jackson, too, had first come to India on military service; he had climbed in Kashmir, Ladakh and Nepal, and in addition had had four Alpine seasons. MacKinnon had had fourteen Alpine seasons, and been to the Himalayas twice. Hardie, a New Zealander, had profited from the splendid advantage enjoyed by his countrymen, that of having right at the door a real wilderness of fine mountains. He was an expert on snow and ice, less interested in rock. He had been once to the Himalayas, to the Barun in 1954. Our chief expert on rock was Joe Brown, whose climbs in Britain and in the Alps had already won him a remarkable reputation. Once, later on, he was heard to call the Kangchenjunga climb a long trudge. But in the end he was not disappointed. He had a particular liking for cracks, especially on overhangs, and, as will be told, he was lucky enough to find what he wanted on the highest pitch of all. George Band, who was with Joe on that occasion, was also a fine rock-climber; he had been on Everest, and the next year on Rakaposhi. John Clegg was an experienced climber, and, as we found, a singer with a stock of good songs.

By March 10th we were all at Rungneet, Mr. and Mrs. Henderson's bungalow outside Darjeeling. From the lawn we looked north to our mountain only forty-six miles away. The Great Shelf, the Gangway, the Sickle, which we had pictured and considered, were there in front of us.

We had not arrived without difficulties. Indeed, I believe that only the kindness of the Himalayan Club enabled us to overcome them. There were moments at Darjeeling when I felt that now half the work of exploring Kangchenjunga was done. Certainly, the bad part was behind us: the anxieties about our baggage, the interminable arguments with minor officials about small points not covered in so many words by the written regulations. For Hardie and MacKinnon there had

12

5 Yalung Camp

6 Yalung Camp   Looking east, across the main va

been a slow, hot, dusty journey across country, watching the baggage-car to see that it was changed from train to train and not left forgotten in a siding. When we arrived, Streather had already been there a week, arranging for the engagement of over three hundred coolies for the march in. In this, his main helper was Ang Yangzin, the wife of Ang Tharkay. She and her husband rounded up every coolie to be had in the bazaars and the neighbouring hills, and thanks to them we had just enough for our needs.

I was the last to arrive at Darjeeling. I had had to go to Sikkim. Shortly before leaving England we had been told that the Government of Sikkim objected to any attempt to climb the mountain. Its eastern side is in Sikkim; its name is Sikkimese, meaning the Five Treasuries of the Great Snow; the Sikkimese regard it as a god and a protector.

At Gangtok I was entertained by the Indian Political Officer, Mr. Apa B. Pant, and through the kind offices of the Dewan, Mr. N. K. Rustomji, had the privilege of talks with H.H. Sir Tashi Namgyal, K.C.S.I., K.C.I.E., Maharajah of Sikkim, and with the Maharaj Kumar, Lt. Col. P. T. Namgyal, P.B., O.B.E. I promised that we would leave the top and its immediate neighbourhood untouched, and would go no farther up the mountain than was necessary to assure us that the top could be reached.

At Darjeeling our Sherpas met us. In charge of them was Dawa Tenzing. He was then, I believe, between forty-five and fifty years old. He had been with me on Himalayan trips for the last three years: in 1952 and 1953 as my personal Sherpa, in 1954 as *sirdar* of the New Zealand Barun Expedition. Tall for a Sherpa, rather dark of skin, and with a longer face and a more serious expression than is usual in a Sherpa, he was one of the few who, in spite of long service with climbing expeditions, had kept his pigtail. On Everest he had twice carried a load to the South Col without oxygen, and reached the Col fit and ready to go farther if need be. He was not only an old friend of mine but an old friend of Tom MacKinnon and of Norman Hardie. I had asked him to choose for the expedition the best of the Sherpas from Sola Khumbu. Some, of course, I had named to him, but in the main he was given a free choice. I wanted Sola Khumbu men because I knew many of them and knew their homes. Some of them met me as soon as I reached Rungneet: Urkien, with his square, bony, intelligent face, a future *sirdar* of the highest class, strong, and now technically skilled in climbing; Aila from Phorche, a huge man for a Sherpa, barrel-chested, his pigtail always dishevelled, his voice deep and loud, useful as a fog-horn to guide lost coolies in mist; Ang Dawa from Kunde, more the typical Sherpa in looks than these others, round-faced, slant-eyed, grinning, physically tough, and given to slapstick comedy; Annullu, Dawa Tenzing's half-brother, broad, strong, and sharp-witted, now sophisticated, with a felt hat and close crop, but still a tireless worker when at it; and Changjup, another old companion, the greatest laugher of all of them. Changjup, too, had succumbed to fashion in shedding his pigtail and his turquoise and coral ear-rings. When I had rebuked him, we sat by their fire, and I heard all their news since we last met. For Norman Hardie and me, to see them again was to resume our life with them where six months before it had been broken off.

There were two ways from Rungneet to Kangchenjunga: we could follow, as Kempe had done, the Singalila ridge almost to Kang Peak, and then cross the Chumbab La and the Semo La into the Yalung, or we could leave the Singalila ridge at Phalut, and travel to the Yalung by the valleys and ridges of the west flank of the Singalila. Kempe had left Darjeeling on April 10th and had found snow on the passes at the north end of the Singalila. Here his coolies had been unequal to the snow and the weather, and there had been desertion. We

14

were leaving Darjeeling four weeks earlier, and we should
have with us over three hundred coolies: almost any detour
would be better than the Singalila ridge route. When Kempe's
party returned in 1954, Gilmour Lewis had come back alone
by a route to the west. From the Yalung he had gone a day's
march downstream and crossed a low pass to the village of
Yamphodin. Thence, keeping well down on the Nepalese
side of the Singalila, he had passed through Khebang, Mehele
and Chyangthapu, and rejoined the Singalila at Phalut. On
his advice, we chose this way in, and had arranged, through
Ajeeba, who had been Kempe's *sirdar*, to have caches of rice
and flour waiting for us along this route: twenty maunds [1] at
Chyangthapu and sixty maunds at Yamphodin. Though the
distance to the mountain in a straight line was only forty-six
miles, our way would be twice as long.

Our last days of preparation coincided with a meeting of
the Darjeeling Planters' Association, and on March 12th they
kindly invited us all to lunch with them at the Planters' Club.
We were going to their particular mountain, the mountain to
which many of them had looked all their lives from the
Darjeeling tea-gardens, and they wished us well. Many of
them were already our friends: Jack and Jill Henderson, whose
house was our home; and Peter Bell and Peter Webster,
themselves climbers, who had helped us to get ready, and were
to take some of us in their cars for the first miles of our march.
They expected me at that lunch, I think, to tell them how we
were going to climb the mountain, but I could not: all I
could do was to thank them for their help and their good
wishes.

We travelled in two parties: seven of us, with Dawa Tenzing,
some of the Sherpas, and two hundred coolies, in the first;
Tom MacKinnon and Tony Streather, with the remainder of
the Sherpas and one hundred coolies, a day later. The march

[1] One maund equals 80 lb. approximately.

took ten days. The first three, to Phalut, were on the crest of the Singalila. Only from there did we have long views of the mountains: Kangchenjunga at dawn spread out widely before us, and once, a glimpse to the north-west of Makalu and the Everest group. It was too early in the season for the rhododendrons to be in full bloom: only here and there did we see a tree in flower, a splash of pink in the dull green forest. Before we left the Singalila, we saw also once or twice tall magnolias, their great white waxen blooms clear on the leafless branches. Once off the Singalila, our way was through intensively cultivated Nepal: Chyangthapu, Mehele, Khebang, Yamphodin. Every square inch of the ground that could be cultivated was terraced, and each night it was on these terraces that we camped. There were now no crops, and we pitched our tents and lit our fires on hard-baked earth.

In a few days we had settled down to the familar pattern of the journey to the mountain. In the morning fires were lit in the cold darkness, and mugs of sweet tea drunk while the camp was being struck and the coolies bustling to be on the move. Then came the best part of the day, the walk before the sun's heat, before the distant views were obscured by haze. Towards eight or nine o'clock came the breakfast halt, when we looked for a stream, and shade to ward off the rays of the sun, now beating uncomfortably on our heads; breakfast was huge, of porridge, bacon or sausage, and eggs, with the unleavened bread of the country, the chapatti, hot, and smeared with butter and marmalade. The afternoons were more leisurely. One by one we sauntered off, our umbrellas up in the heat. Our pace was adapted to the distance the coolies could go in a day; they went in little groups, stopping every few hundred yards to rest their loads on sticks; several times during an afternoon's march we would be an hour or more sitting under the shade of a pipal or banyan tree on a breezy ridge between one valley and the next. At last, never much after four o'clock, the site for the night's camp was chosen, and we were free to take photographs, to fish, or to explore. Supper was the main meal: tinned food, with local vegetables, rice, potatoes, and sometimes greens. The coolies used to scatter from our central camp, and find for themselves shelter among the trees and rocks: a hill-side would become a blaze of small twinkling lights, their cooking-fires, one to each group of half a dozen or so friends. We were usually in bed by nine, and ready at five to begin the next day.

At Chyangthapu our arrival was followed by one of the violent thunderstorms common before the monsoon. We were giving out rice to the coolies from the dump put there by Ajeeba when huge raindrops began to fall and a gusty wind rose. Soon it was dark except for the brilliant flashes of the lightning, the rain was a downpour, and the wind rushed through the great trees by the village, cracking off branches and swaying the tops. All was confusion until the food-depot was moved into an empty hovel, the school, and the distribution could again be started. For this, and to save tents and baggage, all had to turn out, and before we settled in another hovel for supper we were wet to the skin. Next morning was clear and bright again; Phalut, from which we had come down eight thousand feet the day before, was white with snow.

We kept on to the northward, contouring populous slopes, at this season barren, where the Nepalese have denuded the land of trees, and on March 19th, after crossing a particularly airy suspension-bridge, we camped in a downpour below the village of Khebang, where we were royally welcomed next morning. The villagers are mainly high-caste Hindus, and they have joined together to subscribe to the pay of a schoolmaster. The gateway to the village was decorated with flowers for the occasion, and after entering under the arch of flowers, we were treated by the school-children to a concert of Nepali songs. We had our breakfast on a patch of grass in the village. They could

17

see it all. Behind our green ran a low wall; the more privileged or active scrambled onto it and squatted there, a long line, sixty or seventy of them in a row; those less quick off the mark had to stand or squat in front; some moved freely about, seeing us eat now from that side, now from this. We sat there for all to see, on a tarpaulin spread on the ground, while Thondup the cook and his helpers bustled about. Every now and then some of our more officious Sherpas, thinking the watchers were closing in dangerously on their feeding charges, would squeeze between them and us, sweeping them back with waves of the hand: "Gently there, not too close, crowding makes them restless and difficult."

The day was hot, too, and we all had umbrellas up to keep the sun off. It was an experience for everybody. We saw an extraordinary variety of faces, old and young, smooth and lined, and of ornaments and clothing. And what did they see? It would be amusing to know, to read the essays written next day at Khebang school on the subject, 'Visit of English Expedition'. They must have enjoyed the spectacle, because later, when we were at Base Camp, I had a note from the master saying that he would like to visit our camp; but although I wrote back to give him a warm invitation, he did not appear. Perhaps the contrast between his hot village on the dusty slope and the icy barrenness of the upper Yalung was too great for him to face except in a sort of joyous fancy.

That day we had our first glimpse of men from Ghunsa. Rounding a precipitous hill-side above a gorge between Khebang and Yamphodin we came on a group of herdsmen; they looked to us like Sherpas; they had pigtails, Sherpa-style clothes and ear-rings, and broad grins; we immediately felt at home with them, and so did our Sherpas, who talked to them in a language like their own.

At Yamphodin nearly seventy of the little Darjeeling coolies decided that they had had enough, influenced probably by tales told by the Yamphodin men of the rigours of the pass ahead, which rises to 11,000 feet before dropping into the Simbua Khola. We could not persuade them to come on. Instead, we left their loads in the village, to be fetched later.

It was only a short march to our camp above Yamphodin. It was in a jungle-filled gorge, the highest source we had of water, a place of great boulders and rhododendron-thicket. The coolies scattered into the bush, and during a stroll there in the evening I heard one of them singing over his fire. Picking up some of the words, I asked a Sherpa to translate for me. The coolie's song was about a poor Nepali peasant like himself, Tenzing, who climbed to the top of the world, climbed out of his lowly state to fame and wealth.

March 22nd was one of the great days of our walk in. It was a long day, a four-thousand-foot pull up to a grassy saddle leading to the Simbua. On the way, we climbed a hill-side ravaged by a forest fire. Only here and there had a tree been spared, usually a large rhododendron. These solitary trees stood out, a flaring scarlet against the black background of ashes. Above the burnt area was a patch of rather pleasant jungle, with open spaces, and tall sturdy trees, mosses on their trunks; the path wound among the trees and led to a broad meadow, the crest of the pass. We arrived just in time to see over. Behind us were tall firs; before us, northwards, the far side plunged into the wooded lower gorge of the Simbua, and up to our right we saw the valley of Yalung. Most of it was already hidden by morning cloud, but one peak stood out, to the left of the valley as we looked, a wedge of rock plastered with ice and snow, Jannu.

It was very lovely coming down into the Simbua from the pass. The extra height and the north-facing slope lent the valley a freshness lacking in the hotter, duller valleys behind us. There was snow in drifts on the track as it wound down through the rhododendrons; most of the trees here were not

19

yet in flower. By evening we were at the river, and looking for a place to camp. We were at 10,000 feet, and it was colder that night than since we had left Phalut.

Next day I wanted to get as far up the valley as we could before camping, because we were going that day to what would be our first permanent camp. The only guide we had to where to put it was Kempe's account of the valley; we planned to push on as far as we could, and to look round for something that would suit us. We started early: I was out at four-thirty waking the coolies, to get their fires going, and two hours later the whole caravan was on the move. It sounds a long time, but it is hard with a party this size to be any faster. Food has to be cooked and eaten, a business at which no Indian is willing to be hurried; tents have to be taken down and packed for the road; loads have to be tied together by the coolie in just the way that suits him, lifted onto his back, and carried out of camp; then you think, "There's one load gone", but no, it is dumped a few yards on, all ready, and back he comes, to squat near, having a last cigarette before starting up the trail. The first men may make their real start an hour after waking, but not those who have gone for the night perhaps half a mile into the woods to find a sheltering cave.

It was a hot morning, a glorious walk. We were going up a narrow valley wooded with firs. The fir needles under our feet gave a wonderful smell in the heat of the sun; here and there were cushions of pink primula, and rhododendrons flowering early; the Simbua or Yalung river gurgled at our feet. Every now and then we came to a clearing beside it, where there was a wide grassy level, and a view of peaks up the valley: rocky spurs, now snow-covered, above Tseram, and farther away the real mountains, Ratong Peak and Kabru, their bulging ice gleaming in the morning sun above the small clouds.

At twelve-thirty we reached Tseram, and two hours later, in

mist and lightly falling snow, we came to a grassy shelf where there was a small ruined Buddhist temple.[1] We were assured by some of the Sherpas that this was the site of Kempe's Base Camp, which we later found had been some way up the valley; in any case, our last coolies were a long way behind, and there was little hope of going farther today. It seemed a pleasant spot, where there was an unlimited supply of firewood close at hand, and I decided to make it our camp for the next month.

[1] The name of this place is uncertain. It may be Dachenrol, or Decherol, Monastery; the Ghunsa men said it was called Yalung, though on the *Survey of India* maps Yelung is farther downstream. I have called it Yalung Camp.

CHAPTER THREE

THE YALUNG VALLEY

March 6th–April 5th

THE shelf is of about an acre, at 13,000 feet, on the right bank of the valley. There, when our stores were piled, we paid off our Darjeeling coolies. After our arrival, on the afternoon of March 23rd, it continued to snow, and by nightfall the camp was covered. We had seen nothing of our surroundings. This was a pattern of weather constant, with minor variations, during the next few weeks. During the morning, or about noon, cloud began to form, and snow to fall; during the night the snowfall would stop, and as a rule we would wake to find the sky clear, our camp buried in snow. At sunrise, almost at once, the snow would begin to melt; first it ran off the tents, then it thinned on the ground; strips of grass appeared; by noon only a few patches were left in shadowed places.

After our first night we saw where we were. For five thousand feet above us, the mountain-side rose to the ridge that separates the Yalung from the valley of Ghunsa to the west; low down, the slopes were covered by berberis, scrub juniper, and dwarf rhododendron; higher up they were bare and rocky. Below camp there was a moraine crest, beyond which the slope fell steeply to the valley floor, to Tseram, a thousand feet down. Here the valley was well wooded, and the trees, rhododendron, fir and juniper, grew to within a few hundred feet of our camp, forest on which we were now to rely for fuel for all camp-fires. Straight across the valley to the east were two rock peaks of about 18,000 feet, plastered with new snow; they hid from us

22

the region of the Kang La and the north end of the Singalila ridge. Two hundred yards farther up the valley was the terminal moraine of the Yalung glacier, three or four hundred feet high and half a mile wide. In that direction our view was cut off, on the left, by a ridge which ran down to the east from Boktoh, the southernmost peak on the west wall of the Yalung; but over the top of the terminal moraine, to the north-east, we could see something of the east wall of the valley: first, Ratong Peak, a blunt conical mountain of ice, and, farther north, Kabru, a long ridge which from here looked like a succession of snow-domes, all of about equal height, whose glaciers seemed to hang above the Yalung. Kangchenjunga was hidden.

Our plan now was to ferry loads up the Yalung to a base camp at the foot of the mountain, and we expected that with the numbers at our disposal, which included fifty Sherpas and Sherpa coolies, this would take us about a month. We did not know where we should put our permanent base. It would, we thought, have to be somewhere near the foot of Kempe's Buttress; and the first task was to explore the valley, in order to choose the site, and the porters' route. At the same time we wanted to measure the heights of features on the Yalung face of the mountain, and to visit Ghunsa village to buy meat, vegetables, and grain. In our first week, therefore, Band, Jackson and Mather went to Ghunsa with Annullu; MacKinnon and I went up the Yalung to look for a base; Hardie and Brown came with us to make a survey of the face and to measure the heights on it; and Streather and Clegg stayed at Yalung Camp, to follow us up the valley, bringing with them the first convoy of coolies.

From the top of Kangchenjunga to the beginning of the Simbua Khola below the terminal Yalung moraine, the Yalung valley is about sixteen miles long; and it is about four miles wide. The glacier in its floor is half to three-quarters of a mile wide, and twelve miles long: starting below the Talung Saddle, it stretches for about three miles west to the 'Corner', and then for over four miles south before gently swinging south-west for the rest of its course. It is a typical Himalayan glacier, in retreat, rough, rubble-covered and ugly, withdrawn from its moraines and therefore difficult of access. On both banks there are lateral moraines, and between them and the mountains are some pleasant ablation valleys; but these moraines do not extend for all the length of the glacier; in places the ice is bordered by rocky bluffs which form the valley's sides, and in other places there are tributary glaciers. Where there is a lateral moraine, its crest is two to four hundred feet above the general level of the glacier, and the side of the moraine next the glacier is a face of grit and boulders embedded in solid mud at an angle of sixty to seventy degrees.

Above Yalung Camp, on the right bank, an ablation valley runs up for six miles. Here and there it opens out into pastures several acres in extent; between these it is sometimes a narrow stony defile, but one pasture is so large and flat that there is there a shallow lake half a mile long. The highest of these pastures is called by the Ghunsa men 'Octong'; above it, the ablation valley is narrower for a quarter of a mile, and filled with boulders; then it disappears, where the lateral moraine joins the steep face of a spur of Boktoh. Half a mile above Octong the Tso glacier enters from the west; above it is another short ablation valley which we did not visit but which was the site of Crawford and Raeburn's 'Tso Camp' of 1920, and probably of one of the camps of the 1905 expedition. Because of the retreat of the tributary Tso glacier, to reach this valley would now be difficult, and, except by a long detour on the main glacier, dangerous. It is the highest ablation valley on the right bank of the Yalung: north of it the glacier is bordered by steep rock and hanging ice. On the left bank of the main glacier opposite Octong there is no ablation valley; here also

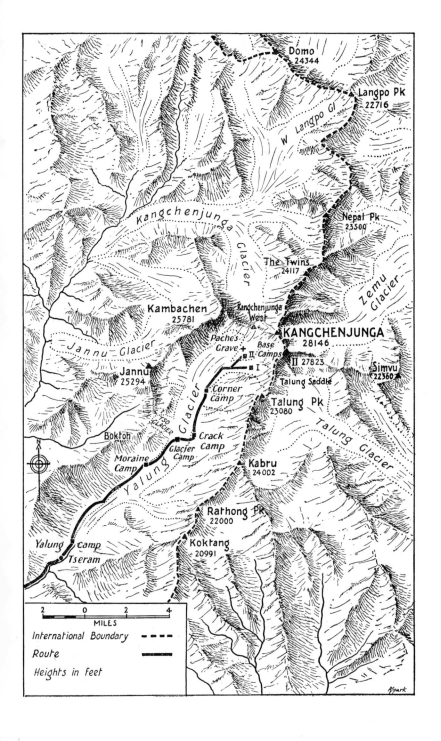

Domo
24344

Langpo Pk
22716

W Langpo Gl

Nepal Pk
23500

Kangchenjunga Glacier

The Twins
24117

Zemu Glacier

Kambachen
25781

Kangchenjunga
West

KANGCHENJUNGA
28146

Pache's
Grave

Base
Camps
II
I

II 27823

Simvu
22360

Jannu Glacier

Talung Saddle

Jannu
25294

Corner
Camp

Talung Pk
23080

Boktoh

550
Glacier

Crack
Camp

Glacier
Camp

Talung Glacier

Moraine
Camp

Kabru
24002

Yalung Glacier

Rathong Pk
22000

Yalung camp
Tseram

Koktang
20991

2   0   2   4
MILES

International Boundary - - -

Route ———

Heights in feet

A.Spark

the glacier is bordered by steep rock and hanging ice, the base of Ratong Peak and of the southerly buttresses of Kabru; but north of the entry of the Tso glacier, there is on the left bank a small ablation valley, the site of Raeburn's Nao Camp, a sheltered hollow. North of it again, a tributary glacier comes in from the east, from Talung Peak and Kabru, joining the main glacier only a short way below the Corner. At the Corner, beyond the tributary glacier, the ablation valley reappears once more, for a short distance; thereafter, on the south bank, the north face of Talung Peak plunges in cliffs of rock and ice straight to the main glacier.

The Corner is made by a spur of rock that runs west from Talung. Here the main glacier is about three-quarters of a mile across. Above, it splays out, and has two main tributaries: on the north, the ice from Jannu and from the ridge between Jannu and Kangchenjunga West; and on the east the ice from Talung Saddle and from Kangchenjunga.

We found at once that to carry up the Yalung glacier was more difficult than we had expected. At the first attempt it took us three days to reach the Corner, and except for one day spent in an exploration we went on this occasion no farther. On each of the three days we plodded up through new snow, unable, where there was a track, to see it. On the third day in particular, coming up the ablation valley below the Corner, we floundered sometimes thigh-deep where the snow hid the holes between the boulders lying on the steep hill-side. For the porters it was very heavy going, and we found that, although we gained little height, two miles was generally a full day's march. We placed our first camp in the middle of the glacier, Glacier Camp, half-way between Octong and the small ablation valley on the left bank, and our second camp at the lower end of that ablation valley. This is the site of Kempe's Boulder Camp, but was known to us as Crack Camp: there is a boulder here twenty feet high, in the side of which is a

26

thin overhanging crack which was climbed by Joe Brown on his first arrival. This first exploration taught us that from Yalung Camp to Glacier Camp was too far a carry, and from Glacier Camp to Crack Camp too short; and we made a camp at Octong, called Moraine Camp. From Yalung Camp to Moraine Camp, the first day's journey, was nearly six miles, from Moraine Camp to Crack Camp was two miles, and from Crack Camp to Corner Camp was two and a quarter miles. That we looked on these as equivalent days shows the relative difficulty of the ground. The worst section on the whole route was not far above Moraine Camp. From the meadow where we pitched our tents we climbed over boulders to the crest of the moraine, here sharp. From the crest, the eastern slope fell to the glacier at an angle of sixty degrees, two hundred feet of grey mud and grit in which stones and boulders of all sizes were loosely embedded. Every few minutes there was a clatter as a stone worked loose and tumbled to the glacier, followed by a rush of smaller pebbles. The lower half of the wall was scored into steep parallel gullies where these stones had worn their ways down, and the foot of it was like the shore of a sea, a line up and down the edge of the glacier, as far as the eye could reach, of stones large and small.

The walk over the glacier to Crack Camp was very laborious, and often dull. Ridge after ridge of ice, covered with boulders, had to be crossed; wide detours had to be made to avoid lakes and ice-cliffs; the way at first was on loose stones covered with new snow; and towards the end of the journey there was for a short distance some danger, we never knew how much, from avalanches falling from the hanging glaciers of Kabru. On the morning of March 28th, when Streather and Clegg were at Glacier Camp with a party of Sherpas, I was on my way up to Corner. I was resting for a moment, when far up and to my left, as I looked back down the valley, there was a sudden sharp 'crack'. An ice-cliff was breaking off Kabru. I watched

27

the avalanche thunder down into the Yalung behind me, and break into a billowing white cloud which crossed our track of the day before and travelled fast towards Glacier Camp. As it went, its clouds of ice-particles grew huge, Glacier Camp was hidden by them, and they swept on towards the far side of the Yalung, a mile away. Surely, I thought, it must just be cloud; Glacier Camp lay behind so many ridges, which yesterday we had crossed with such labour, that it must be safe from any blocks of a size to do serious harm; but all the same, they must have had a monumental blast of wind there, and perhaps tents blown down. Later Streather told me that they had noticed that they were suddenly in cloud, and that a little snow fell, but that was all, and Clegg, asleep in his bag, had not even wakened.

It was March 28th when for the first time MacKinnon, Hardie, Brown and I reached Corner Camp. We had come up after a day of blizzard, over slopes covered with deep soft snow. We camped in the funnel-shaped ablation valley, just short of the turn of the Corner; and while camp was being pitched we climbed the lateral moraine to get a view. From a point between Yalung Camp and Moraine Camp we had seen the upper part of the mountain: part of the Upper Icefall, the Great Shelf, and the Gangway. The lower part we had never seen. It was a windy afternoon, the wind blowing powder snow about the camp; but it stayed fine later than usual, and round the Corner we had our view: the whole ten thousand feet of the south-west face of Kangchenjunga, rising from the glacier less than two miles away.

We were now closer under the face, and it was fore-shortened: the Gangway and the Great Shelf looked less steep than they had looked from down the valley. But it was our first near view of the two icefalls, and they looked steep and long. We saw well, too, Kempe's Buttress, and it seemed from here to end far below the top of the Lower Icefall. To the left,

7 Ghunsa

8 The Yalung glacier   Above Moraine Camp, looking towards Crack and Corner Cam

to the west of the Lower Icefall, the site of Pache's Grave and
the slopes above it leading to the top of the Western Buttress
were in full view, and it looked, had we not known that it was
not so, as if above Pache's Grave there was a straight route
right up to the lower part of the Upper Icefall. The inter-
ruption, the steep east wall of the Western Buttress, did not
show from here. It was easy to understand that to Crowley's
party this must have seemed the direct way towards the Great
Shelf. As it was, we paid those slopes little attention, our
interest being all in the Lower Icefall, and the route to where
we hoped to pitch our base camp at its foot.

Next morning was fine, and we split the party. Hardie
took a theodolite up onto the spur of Talung Peak to mark out a
base line and measure from there the heights of the West Col
of Kangchenjunga, of the Great Shelf, of the middle of the
Upper Icefall, of the foot of it, and of the top and bottom of
Kempe's Buttress. With him he took Brown and Urkien. I
chose two Sherpas, Ang Temba and Namche Ang Dawa, to
come with MacKinnon and me to look for a way to a base
camp. The rest of the Sherpas we sent down to Glacier Camp
to bring up some of the loads dumped there by Streather.

My party was off at eight-thirty, forty minutes after the sun
had touched our camp. We rounded the Corner, and ploughed
our way down through snow two feet deep to the glacier four
hundred feet below. From the Corner we saw this glacier clearly.
Starting from the névée under Talung Saddle and under the
cliffs below the south end of the Great Shelf, it flowed towards
us smoothly until it was joined by the ice of the Lower Icefall.
From the junction downwards, its northern third was widely
and deeply crevassed, its centre was rough with ridges and
pinnacles, and its southern third was smooth, a comparatively
unbroken trough, which would have offered an attractive
route to its upper reaches were it not for the hanging glaciers
stuck on the face of Talung Peak high above it and the debris

of avalanches scattered on its floor. We decided to avoid this trough at all costs, and first sought a route up the centre of the glacier out of range of the Talung avalanches. MacKinnon and I took it in turns to plough the trail and pick the way; the Sherpas carried the sacks. First we crossed from the foot of our moraine to the centre of the glacier. It was a 'dry' glacier, that is, one of which the ice in summer is ordinarily bare, but it was covered now with six inches of new snow, which hid its crevasses, so that almost from the beginning we made use of the rope. The going at first was straightforward, but very laborious; it was scorching hot, our faces burned, and, unacclimatized as we were, we panted hard, and our throats became dry and sticky. We turned, when well out on the glacier, to find a way up its centre. Soon we were in a maze of ice-pinnacles, and then were facing a succession of transverse ridges of ice; here and there were crevasses whose general direction was across our left front, and which therefore forced us again and again farther to our right. After nearly six hours we had reached a point level with the Western Buttress; we were not more than two hundred yards in a straight line from the place where we wanted to put our base camp, and we sat on an ice-ridge to look at the ground. Immediately in front of us was a deep crevasse, too wide to bridge, which stretched to the right towards the trough under Talung, and on the left ended in a maze of ice-pinnacles and chasms. It looked as if we might possibly cross it there; but beyond it was another of the same kind, and beyond that another, and another. It was two-fifteen, and we were very tired, too tired to do any more that day without exhausting ourselves more than was right at this early stage of the expedition. We came down.

In two and a half hours we reached camp; we dragged ourselves into our tents and lay drinking sweet tea and lemon, too tired even to enjoy that, and too tired to face the thought of supper. This is what is usual during the early stage of acclimatization: a degree of fatigue that can be borne with patience only because the climber knows that the phase does not last, and that in a week's time, when he returns to camp after a spell of hard work, though tired, he will not be exhausted, but ready after a short rest to eat, and then to do more if need be.

We had learnt a lot. It was evident that our Sherpa coolies and Ghunsa men could not yet stock a base camp; the route was too difficult for them; they were not equipped for it, nor for the weather we were having; we should have, first, to wait, stocking meantime Corner Camp as a preliminary base, and then to rely mainly on our permanent Sherpas, who were equipped for ice-climbing, to carry farther.

Since Hardie and Brown still had some surveying to do, we thought we would let them complete it next day, March 30th, while MacKinnon and I rested, and then on the following day would all go up towards our future base camp, partly as an outing, to acclimatize a little more, and also here and there to improve the route.

But in the morning there was wind. We had heard it the day before, blowing over Talung Saddle with a continuous roar which at first we mistook for an avalanche, until we realized that it went on continuously for hours; and we had from down valley seen it sweeping the clouds across the upper face of the mountain from west to east. We had not yet had much of it in our camp; but when we woke the tents were flapping and banging hard, and the snow was driving past us at each fierce gust. We lay there, snug in our bags, listening to it. After a while I began to think it stronger than any wind I had known before, and I wondered about the safety of the tents. Hardie wanted to start out to finish his survey, though it hardly seemed that a theodolite could be relied on to be still in such a wind as this. Moreover, far from showing any sign of slackening as the morning wore on towards sunrise, the strength of the wind grew, until suddenly my tent was lashed with a strip of cloth

31

and Hardie shouted from outside, "The big Dome's gone". I pulled on a pair of gym-shoes and hurried out. There was no sign of the Dome. Where it had been were two small sleeping-bags, shut and curled. As I watched, they opened carefully; two Sherpa faces peered out, and then, seeing the sky above, withdrew, and the bags were shut again, their draw-cords tight.

Not all the Sherpas were so unconcerned. Changjup, close to me, was hanging on to the gable-end of a large green Meade tent which had torn along the length of its ridge and along one of its eaves; it threatened every moment to tear further, or to be carried away; with presence of mind he cut both windward guys and collapsed the gable, ignoring the protests of those inside. Leaving him, I went with Joe Brown to look for the Dome. Since there was no sign of it, we went in the direction of the wind. The valley rose a hundred feet, narrowed, and beyond the Corner, two hundred yards from camp, fell slightly. Here we found the remains of the Dome, crumpled, its poles bent. It had been carried clear of the ground, and dropped in a small hollow.

Between us we took it back, by which time our feet were numb; it was still before sunrise, the wind as strong as ever, the temperature below zero. Guying down our tents more firmly, we went into them again to discuss our plans. It was clear that even Corner Camp must wait a little for occupation. We would dump everything here, make a cache of the tents under a boulder, and retire for a few days to await some improvement in the weather. Only Hardie would stay here: his survey was still not finished, and if one or two of us stayed, it would seem less like defeat and demoralization. So he remained there two more nights with Urkien, while the rest of us returned to Yalung Camp.

It had taken us three days to come up; we went down in one. We found a small dump of stores at Crack Camp, and

32

9 The Yalung glacier   *Left* On the way to Crack Camp

Right On the way to Corner Camp

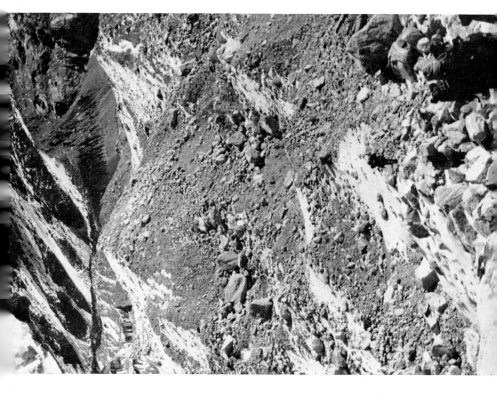

saw that the Sherpas had been writing 'Om Mani Padme Hum'
in huge letters on the face of the boulder there. We left at
eight-thirty, and in two and a half hours from Corner Camp
we reached Glacier Camp; the few Sherpas temporarily living
there were starting up for Crack Camp when we arrived.
Already the track across the glacier was beginning to be better
marked. Many more cairns had been built. The biggest
change was at the descent to the glacier, above Moraine Camp.
There, where before we had sidled precariously across the
loosest imaginable slope, with threatening boulders above us,
Streather and Clegg had found a gully which went straight
down from top to bottom of the wall, and had cleared it of
large stones at the top, and fixed there two hundred feet of rope.
At the end of the rough walk down, it was a hard pull up, even
with the rope as a handrail to haul on; but it was safe and
straightforward. Streather met us here at one-thirty, on his way
to live at Crack Camp. Dawa Tenzing was with him, and we arranged that in the days to come there should be ten Sherpas
with Streather at Crack, carrying up to Corner, another ten at
Moraine, carrying up to Crack, and twenty at Yalung, carrying
up to Moraine.

So far, none of us had been very high. MacKinnon and I had
reached about 18,000 feet; we had, for the time being, found
it high enough.

The fact of acclimatization has been known since the earliest
Everest expeditions, when it was recognized that it takes several
weeks for men to become fully acclimatized, and that it is
better, until that has happened, to postpone the main effort
on a big peak.[1] We should have liked to spend a week or two

---

[1] 'I am of the opinion that exercise before the climbing begins is of great value.
Mallory and I were the only ones whom Longstaff allowed to make the attempts
on Everest; and we were probably rendered fit in this way by the subsidiary expeditions we had made on the way to Mount Everest and by our preliminary work
in getting the camp ready on the North Col.'

T. H. SOMERVELL in *The Assault on Mount Everest*. Arnold.

33

10 Crack Camp

doing nothing but explore the lower heights; but we could not spare the time. Though we did make a few short expeditions just for training, for the most part we had to become acclimatized in the course of our other preparations.

Going down from Moraine on March 30th we noticed at once the new freshness that came from being now at fifteen instead of at seventeen thousand feet; there was a gentle wind blowing up-valley, bringing a home-like wet mist which condensed on our jerseys, and a little snow. We swung down in the face of the weather, taking for the journey only an hour and forty minutes; walking up four days earlier, we had taken five hours.

Next day we spent at our camp by the ruined temple. Much of the snow had gone, and we could see already how pleasant it would be there, and at Moraine Camp, in six weeks' time. We were expecting the return of our Ghunsa party, and in the evening they appeared; they said that the headman of Ghunsa was collecting twenty-five maunds of food for us, and that the first lift of this food was on its way. The same day, Hardie came down, and presently handed me a list of the heights on the Yalung face: the col between Kangchenjunga and Kangchenjunga West, over 27,500 feet; the top of the Great Shelf, over 25,000; a rock on a level with the centre of the Upper Icefall, 22,000; the top of Kempe's Buttress, 19,500; and the foot of it about 18,000.

We were pleased with some of the figures: it was good news that the top of the Great Shelf was so high, since this shortened the formidable slopes above; and it was good news, too, that the Upper Icefall was so low; we had guessed its general height to be about a thousand feet higher, which would have made our difficulties there greater. It was disappointing to know that our base camp would be below 18,000 feet, and that the top of Kempe's Buttress was at only 19,500; we had supposed that it was more than a thousand feet higher; but now, at least, we were on firm ground and were unlikely to be frustrated by serious mistakes in altitude and distance.

The Ghunsa men with our food were a day late, arriving at evening on April 2nd. They had crossed a pass to the north of us, and dumped their loads between us and Moraine Camp before coming down to Yalung to look at us. They were travelling light, each in a dark, often black, Sherpa-style Tibetan coat; on their feet were leather-soled cloth knee-boots; they wore baggy grey woollen breeches, and all had ear-rings and queer hats, ranging from fur-trimmed Tibetan hats to the oldest and most tattered felt hats imaginable. They came trotting down the track at dusk, cheerful, curious, ragged and tough. After a quick inspection of us and our belongings, they went in a body over to the ruined temple, pulled some long timbers off the roof, lashed them together, and set them up at a little distance from our tents, throwing over them a spare tent-cloth that we gave them. Very soon there was a fire inside, and the mass of steaming bodies was crowded round it, enveloped in the acrid juniper smoke that filled every corner and came billowing out under the cloth's edges.

Two days later, Dawa Tenzing and I took stock of the stores still here. Already more than one hundred and fifty loads had gone up the valley, and we had come to the stage of counting what was left and working out how many days it would be before this camp was cleared.

CHAPTER FOUR

THE ROUTE TO BASE CAMP

April 6th–April 14th

NEXT day, on April 6th, Mather and I went up to Moraine Camp. This was now our largest camp. Shelters had been built with tarpaulins and ration-boxes for the low-altitude Sherpas and the Sherpa coolies. Though there was snow outside, these shelters were snug: there were fires in them, and the ground was thickly carpeted with dry grass.

Band and Clegg had gone for the day to Crack, and after a while I walked up to the crest of the moraine to meet the coolies coming down. Waiting at the top of the fixed rope, I could at first see nothing of them. It was snowing hard, and misty, and where they were not hidden by the roughness of the glacier their grey, patched clothes could not easily be seen against the background of grey snow and mottled dark stone. At last I picked out a small group far up, coming down fast along the foot of the moraine wall, where we had told them that they must not come because of the chance of stonefall. Presently I shouted to them, and they halted to look for the author of the voice. They have eyes like hawks, and not only spotted me but knew who it was and called my name. I shouted again; there was a burst of laughter, and they came on to the foot of the fixed rope. Band and Clegg, they said, were coming down, but later.

I followed the coolies into camp, and found that the mail runners had arrived. We had four of these, and sent them off in pairs at weekly intervals. The round journey to Darjeeling and back used to take them about two weeks, and in this way we had a weekly delivery and a weekly collection of mail throughout the expedition.

This mail had in it an important package for me. When I had passed through Delhi, the Indian Air Force had very kindly offered to send me photographs of the south and west faces of the mountain, taken from the air. These now came, with a note from F/Lt. N. D. Jayal, I.A.F., himself a mountaineer, to say that he hoped we should think them more promising than he did. The meaning of his message was soon plain. We had never supposed this mountain easy, but we had thought, from photographs already seen, that on the west ridge, if we could reach it from the top of the Gangway, there might be some freedom of movement to right or to left by which obstacles might be avoided. These pictures showed us a knife-edge, jagged, from which the slopes seemed to fall on both sides precipitously. Only on the south did there seem to be a few breaks in the face below the crest, and these seemed unapproachable except over what looked like the smoothest of steep slabs. Late that evening I showed the pictures to Band, Mather and Clegg. They took them with the optimism that makes climbers always suppose that there must be a way somewhere. Then, as they looked at them, there was silence, followed by little comment.

Next day Mather and I were at Crack Camp by noon. It was snowing when we arrived, and we found the camp empty; Streather and MacKinnon were up at Corner with the Sherpas. They returned in high spirits; they now had fifteen Sherpas working over the route to Corner, under the old pirate Annullu, who looked, as usual, attractively confident and full of fight. For the next two days, Streather and I were to live at Corner; MacKinnon and Mather would then join us.

We moved up in the morning, and instead of camping at the old site, where we had been blown away, we went farther on, round the Corner, where there was more shelter, and where we were in full view of the face of the mountain. We carried up there the tents we had cached last time, and set up also the Dome which had blown away, rigging it this time only half as high as it had been before, and weighing it well down with stones, meaning to use it as a cookhouse.

It had been a finer day than usual, but when I went out at five-thirty for our evening radio call, it was misty and snowing lightly, small dry flakes that did not stick to my windproof clothing. We had a regular routine for radio calls. At arranged times, in the morning or the evening, someone at each camp would put on his eiderdown coat, drag his canvas covers over his eiderdown socks, and crawl out of the tent to make the call from a prominent point nearby. Reception was usually better if we could talk from the crest of a moraine, a place in more or less direct view of the distant camp. There we would brush the snow off a boulder to make a seat, screw in the aerial of the set, adjust once more our woollen gloves, and then start calling "Hullo, Moraine Camp. Hullo, Moraine Camp. Corner Camp calling Moraine. Can you hear me? Over." This time I was a couple of minutes early, and after switching on I sat hunched up, back to the wind, looking out over the glacier hundreds of feet below. It was remote beyond anything I had seen. Occasionally there was the rumble and splash of a stone falling into one of its lakes, or the thunder of an avalanche off Jannu; but mainly there was just silence. In all our wanderings we only touched the edge of the great glacier, saw only from a distance its mazes of grey boulders, ice, and grit. I wondered if any place could seem more indifferent to living beings than this cold ravine. I looked at our small camp in the hollow beneath me. Already, every box we had brought was half buried in snow, formed by the wind into a long streamlined tail, like the snow behind the stones on the slopes above. All at once the radio crackled, "Hullo, Corner. Hullo, Corner"; Crack Camp was on the air. We never lingered for small talk on these calls; at least one of the callers was always in a piercing wind. This time I asked MacKinnon to come up with Mather in the morning to stay, and told him that Streather and I would be spending next day looking once more for a route to a base camp.

The sun came here at twenty minutes past seven, earlier than at our first Corner Camp, and we moved off before eight-thirty. The route we took was much the same as on the day when MacKinnon and I had come, but in a few places, knowing now where we were going, we straightened it out. Going up the centre of the glacier, we found four boulders, each about thirty feet high, in a straight line along our route, and standing at intervals of about three hundred yards. Later, we found them useful as guides to the way home in thick weather, and on the most westerly of them, the biggest, built a cairn. It marked the first long halt for porters carrying up to the base camp, and was our place for putting on the rope. By noon we had reached the farthest point reached by MacKinnon and me on our first visit. We sat on a long hump-backed ridge beyond which was the first of the big crevasses. Just below us, a narrow flake of ice bridged the crevasse obliquely, joining the other side fifty yards to our left. We crossed by cutting along it, sweeping away as we went the masses of powder snow which hid the ice, stone, or chasm beneath. We were now in the broken zone at the north end of another broad ridge. In front of us was another crevasse, which could be crossed by cutting steps down to a boulder jammed between its walls, a route which was later worked out by Brown and adopted by us all; but beyond that crevasse were other and larger crevasses, and today we thought it better to bear right, along the length of the ridge we were on, until, rather nearer than we liked to Talung Peak, we found a place to cross and could bear away to the left once more, in the direction of the foot of Kempe's Buttress. It seemed that we were now past the difficulties, but that the route we had

39

followed through the crevasses might be too hard for the porters. It was two-thirty, and, sure that there was a way to our base, we turned down to see if there was any alternative to the zig-zag we had just made. There was, in the trough towards the left bank of the glacier, and we followed it down; but it took us through great piles of ice-avalanche debris which had fallen off Talung Peak, and we decided that it would not do; a route must be made among the crevasses.

Back at Corner Camp, we explained to Mather and MacKinnon where we had been, and it was arranged that they should go up in the morning, to work on the route through the crevasses and to follow on right through to our proposed base, where they would pick a safe site for the tents.

These days were very different from those of our first visit to Corner. Then we had been ill-acclimatized, weak, scorched raw by the sun, shivering when cold and tired, unable to eat; now, after only a fortnight, we seemed to be so burned that we could burn no more, leathery; we were thinner, even gaunt, but toughened so that the long day's plod was merely hard work. Heat and cold were no longer enemies which sapped our strength and might drain us of life, but only two more nuisances, to be laughed at with the Sherpas, who stood out in the snow, the flakes white on their jerseys, making Sherpa jests about this unspeakable mountain.

Streather went down to Moraine next day to help speed up the work there, while from Corner Camp I watched the progress of Mather and MacKinnon through binoculars. It was the third, and last, exploration of the route to the base camp. In an hour and a half they had reached the first boulder, and in two hours fifty minutes they were at the big crevasses, improving on our time of yesterday by forty minutes. This was cheering: the route was becoming easier. It stayed fine for longer than the day before, and at three-thirty I could still see them dodging in and out among the ice-ridges. They were back in camp at

11 On the way to Base Camp 1   The Upper and Lower Icefalls on the left, the Great Shelf and the Great Buttress in the centre, and the Talung Cwm on the right

five with good news: they had found a site for Base, and found there some rusty tins, the remains of Kempe's second base camp. They had improved many sections of the route, and were confident that it could be made easily passable for Sherpas; though some time was to elapse, and much work be done, before John Jackson could say of it, as he later did, "You could wheel a pram along it."

It was now time for us to occupy Base, and George Band came up to Corner on this day to go there with me in the morning to stay. In the morning, however, snow was falling heavily, and we postponed the move. Instead, we all went down towards Crack, in the falling snow, to break trail for up-coming Sherpas, and to show them the way. Plastered white, the hooded figures struggled into camp through new snow several inches deep. On Tuesday, April 12th, Band and I occupied Base with Tashi and Changjup. The grind up was hot; there were few clouds that morning, and the glare of the snow was troublesome. We arrived at one-thirty, and after pitching the tents, we sat outside them on boxes. Through a thick shirt over a string vest, I could feel the heat of the sun like that of a hot fire close by. The camp was on ice, into which everywhere stones were frozen; over all was a covering of powdery snow. To right and left, low ridges protected the site from rolling avalanche debris, and east of it the ground sloped gently down away from us to a shallow lake, beyond which it rose again gently towards the head of the valley. We were at about 18,000 feet, on a flat bottom walled in by heights on three sides. To the north-east five thousand feet of rock, bare and brown, rose sheer to the greenish ice-cliffs at the edge of the Great Shelf; to the north was the Lower Icefall, with its flanking rock buttresses; to the east was the icefall from Talung Saddle; and to the south was the north face of Talung Peak, where, far above us, smooth shoots of ice gleamed between the bulges of the hanging glaciers. It was fierce and beautiful;

41

12 From Corner Camp *See Fig.* 1

and our camp seemed set on an island of safety. One shoot on Talung, a polished, twisting gully three thousand feet long, we christened the Cresta Run. It ended not far below our level in the trough on the Talung side of the main glacier.

Soon after the others had started down it began to snow again, but we did not mind: at last there was cloud between us and the sun, and in our tents we were comfortable. Every now and then there was a rumbling roar, and an avalanche plunged down somewhere into the valley, from the Great Shelf, from the Talung Icefall, or from the direction of the Cresta Run. Many of the falls seemed to come from Talung Peak, and we were glad that we had kept away from it: we had now no anxiety about the party returning to Corner. Band began to mark up on the wall of the tent each avalanche as it fell.

It snowed hard in the night, and was still snowing next morning. We could see only about a hundred yards, and the little tents were weighed down with snow, which we could hear pattering on the canvas. We had to stay where we were. We read, and Band kept up his reckoning of avalanches. During the morning conditions became rather worse; the tent shook and cracked in the wind, which screamed past the guy-ropes as I had thought it did only on the stage; by noon Band's count of avalanches had reached forty-eight, that is, a big one rather more often than once every half hour; under all these noises was the dull roar of the wind over Talung Saddle, a continuous booming noise like that of a great waterfall. To go outside was an expedition, and a disagreeable one. We put on the whole bulk of our warm and windproof clothing, crawled through the sleeve entrance, having first shaken it so as not to spill into the tent any of the snow heaped above, and picked our way through the fresh drifts, trying not to stub our soft-covered toes on hidden stones. All around was wind and desolation.

There was no let-up that day, and in the evening, when I went a hundred yards down from camp to the crest of a low ridge to make our five-thirty radio call, I could see nothing down valley. Floundering about on the ridge, trying to improve the reception by changing my position, I put my foot through an unsuspected crevasse. I seemed a long way from the tents. When I crawled back in, Band swept the snow off my shoulders as I entered, and we settled down for the night, hoping that the morning would be fine enough for us to look at Kempe's Buttress.

April 14th dawned bright. The sun, rising over the south ridge of the mountain, to the left of Talung Saddle, reached us at seven-five. The wind still roared over the saddle, but the sky was perfectly clear and it looked like being a fine day. New powder snow lay all around our camp, dazzling white in the sun, and blown about by the angry gusts in small travelling spirals.

We looked up at Kempe's Buttress. From here it was foreshortened, and though its first part seemed sheer, its upper part looked much less formidable than it had done from Corner. For the time being it was plastered with new snow, as were the huger cliffs under the Great Shelf, cliffs so steep that no snow can rest on them; what snow we saw there was frozen to the rock.

Last year Kempe's party, after showing that there was no safe route by way of the Talung Cwm, had camped where we were now, and had climbed three-quarters of the way up the Lower Icefall. Later, they had found that they could go higher by climbing the rock buttress which forms its left bank, Kempe's Buttress. Their highest camp, estimated then at 21,000 feet, had been on top of this buttress. From it they had been able neither to get a lodgement on the upper part of the Lower Icefall, nor to work through to the right, past the dangerous ice-cliffs which overhang the gullies between

43

Kempe's Buttress and the cliffs below the Great Shelf. A study of their reports had led me to think that it was a case of Kempe's Buttress, and a route through the Lower Icefall from the top of it, or nothing, and we came equipped with ladders for bridging crevasses, and encouraged by the knowledge that in such a place ice is never long at rest, and that what last year was impossible might have become possible now. First we had to find Ron Jackson's route up the rocks to their camp site on top of the buttress.

Band and I set off at eight-thirty. We kept at first up the middle of the glacier, heading roughly for the Talung Cwm. We did not want to go too far right, because of the avalanches off Talung Peak, nor too far up, because of those from the Talung Cwm and the Great Shelf, and we turned left and made for the screes below the east wall of Kempe's Buttress as soon as the complex maze of crevasses at the junction of the Lower Icefall with the main glacier allowed this. Gradually the east wall of the buttress came into view, and we tried to fit in its features with those on a photograph Ron Jackson had given us to show his route. So far we had been walking up a gently inclined, almost unbroken glacier, but now, level with the foot of the buttress, we turned left towards its rocks and crossed a moderately crevassed zone to reach the screes at the foot of the wall. They were snow-covered and laborious to climb. We headed for a bay in the rock-wall five hundred feet above the glacier, the foot of a gully or chimney, where we thought Jackson's route must start. It took us, from camp, two hours to reach it: the fresh snow was treacherous, hiding the loose stones, and the surfaces of scree and slab.

Up in the bay, we put on the rope and again studied Jackson's photographs; we could make out the general structure of the face, but it was hard to pick out the details. Two hundred feet up and to our right was a conspicuous pinnacle on a ridge, which we thought we could identify from the

The Yalung face from the air

See page 57
Photo. Indian Air Force

14 Lower Icefall

Foreground Seracs below the fifty-foot w
Background The Talung Cwm

description; but where was his 'Difficult' chimney which began the climb, and where the traverse over the slabs to another and harder chimney beyond the pinnacle? Immediately above us was an open groove which might have been his first chimney; immediately to our right was a crack in the rocks, leading to a ledge above a slabby wall; this also, we thought, might be it. Both were covered with snow, and we could see on them no holds, nor guess how hard they would be to climb.

First we tried the crack on the right. I held the rope round the shaft of my axe, which was pushed up to the head into rather soft snow, and Band started up. He took a long time; the ledge was only twenty feet away, but every hold had to be found under a layer of snow and cleared of ice before he could use it. At last he was up, silhouetted against the cliffs below the Great Shelf, a long figure balanced on a sloping ledge. After a few minutes he said casually, "I don't like this; I wonder if it is the way." We discussed it. "Well, does it look as if you could get round?" "Hard to say—a bit smooth round there. You'd better come up yourself to have a look." He came down and I took his place. It was more precarious than I had realized, and the glacier seemed suddenly a long way below. "Better look at the other chimney—above you," I said, and turned to come down. When I had watched Band doing so, my feet had been cold, and I had thought he was taking a very long time. I had nearly called out, "Come on, hurry up; you can slide that bit." Now I was glad I had not spoken. Looking up, he grinned, and said, "It's a place, isn't it?" When I was down, he started on the groove-chimney straight ahead, but after going ten feet stuck, and came down: the holds were icy. After a long look round we agreed that this must be the start of the route, and we called it a day. We would give the sun time to work on the snow before coming back with a party to take a camp up the buttress. By one, we were down at Base, and after a rest went on to Corner, where MacKinnon, Mather and Hardie were waiting for us. I spoke on the radio that night to the camps below and asked all but Streather, who was tied to Moraine Camp, waiting for a lift of rations from Ghunsa, to come next day to Corner.

CHAPTER FIVE

THE LOWER ICEFALL

April 15th–April 22nd

ON the evening of April 15th, when all the climbing party but Streather were at Corner, I explained plans, and named my deputy, Norman Hardie.

I wanted Hardie and Band to camp on Kempe's Buttress to find, if they could, a way through the Lower Icefall; Brown, Jackson and Clegg, while continuing to live at Corner, would supervise the ferry of loads to Base, and the setting up of a permanent camp there; MacKinnon and Mather, as soon as the weather allowed, would start for Talung Peak.

In the morning I went down to visit Streather at Moraine, to have a last inspection before dismissing from my thoughts the question of supply from the lower Yalung. The camp was barely recognizable now; there was no snow anywhere, and it was possible to sit on the grass in sunshine and stillness. Only the wind roaring far off over the gap between Kabru and Ratong Peak, as at Base we had heard it roaring over Talung Saddle, recalled the troubles farther up.

I returned to Corner on April 18th. This was for me by far the most anxious time of the expedition. Below the Great Shelf, before we won through to the Upper Icefall, there was always the chance that it might be impossible to avoid the risk of ice-avalanche, and the consequent need to decide whether or not a risk was justifiable. For all of us, indeed, this stage was, I believe, a time of strain; but there was also elation, and anxiety was often forgotten in pleasure at the beauty of the scene, in

47

the happiness of companionship, and in the excitement of finding, bit by bit, the hidden path.

At Corner I found that the lift of loads to Base was going like clockwork: twenty loads a day were being carried there regularly from Corner, and the convoys were taking only three hours to go up and two to come down.

Mather and MacKinnon were at Corner, too. They had been on Talung to a height of about 20,000 feet, and had had to camp in a very much exposed position below a large crevasse which barred their way. They had had a windy night; it had been, Neil Mather said, like sleeping under a railway crossing. Today they had made a further exploration before making a cache of their camp and coming down to Corner for rest.

In the evening I spoke to Hardie on the radio. He and Band were now camped on top of Kempe's Buttress, and had been in the Icefall this afternoon. His report was terse, and not encouraging. They asked for another day, and promised then to show us round.

When we did go up, on April 20th, it was at breakneck speed. We were a large party, MacKinnon, Mather, Brown, Jackson, Clegg, myself, and twenty Sherpas. The route was a highway: the Sherpas had disposed of every ice-obstacle by hacking it down. In one place where, on our first visit, we had climbed a slightly overhanging ten-foot ice-wall, and later put a fixed rope tied to a stake, we found a cutting carved, and it was possible to walk up without even using the hands. Farther on, where we had made a long detour towards Talung Peak, Brown had found that by cutting a corridor to a boulder jammed ten feet down in a crevasse and another corridor up the far side, the route was shortened by fifteen minutes. By twelve-thirty we were at Base, and Jackson and I went on, with Annullu and Urkien. The east wall of Kempe's Buttress was changed; instead of snow-covered slabs and screes, we found bare stones and rough red rocks; here and there were pockets of moss and crumbling earth. We were warm and confident, and there was no wind.

At my previous highest point we found the first fixed rope. We followed it up the steep open chimney directly above, then climbed round to the right over easy slabs, and up a corner, where on our left the rocks overhung, and on our right, smooth and slabby, fell away to the screes. Four hundred feet from the start, we came to a recess; in the floor of it there were boulders, and at the back of it a vertical chimney, twenty feet high, down which hung a rope ladder.

So far the route seemed to tally well with Ron Jackson's description, though to us it seemed harder than he had found it, and there were several places where we should not have cared, as he had put it, to 'scamper down'.

This chimney was the one that Ron Jackson had said was, in climber's jargon, 'Very Difficult', and Hardie and Band had fixed the rope ladder to make it easier for the Sherpas with loads; but even so it was too much for them, and we hauled their sacks up separately.

We were now on a ledge a few feet wide, which ran to the right under a steep wall of rock. Walking that way, we found the wall less steep, and the holds on it good. We scrambled up together, as far as the foot of a long wide snow-gully. We were both rather out of breath, but were feeling fit and thoroughly enjoying this interlude of clean climbing on sound rock.

From the top of the gully we scrambled up a ridge of broken rock, able now to see over to our right, to the east, into the gullies between Kempe's Buttress and the cliffs below the Great Shelf, the gullies down which avalanches fall from the eastern half of the Plateau between the Upper and the Lower Icefalls. Just below the crest of the buttress there was a snow-slope in which platforms for tents had been dug. It was the site of Kempe's highest camp, about fifteen hundred feet above the glacier. While the Sherpas put up our tent we went on

49

a few yards to the top of the buttress to see if there was any sign of Hardie and Band. We found ourselves on a narrow ridge of rock and snow which ended against ice-cliffs above, a prow of rock which divided the stream of the Lower Icefall, part flowing past us on the west, the Lower Icefall proper, and part on the east, where the rocks were so steep that the ice broke off along a line level with us, a line of ice-cliffs, from which it fell down a number of steep gullies to the main glacier.

Looking down Kempe's Buttress, we saw as far as Corner Camp, and looking west, directly across the icefall, here fantastically broken, we saw the east wall of the Western Buttress, several hundred feet high, vertical, and made of poor rock. Hardie and Band were not in sight.

We could see by their steps where they had gone. At our feet was a vertical twenty-foot wall of ice down which they had climbed in a chimney; it led to a bergschrund, a great cleft between the buttress and the icefall. They had crossed this over a number of unstable moth-eaten blocks of ice, between which we could see into black depths. Across the bergschrund the side wall of the glacier was a hundred feet high, and from the foot of it they had slanted up to the right to gain a recess underneath a great overhanging mass of ice shaped like a chandelier. The only way out of the recess was across a vertical wall to the right, by traversing which a more gentle slope could be gained which led back to the left to the top of the overhanging mass above the recess. Now we saw them, coming down that slope. They were only two hundred feet away, but it was half an hour before they joined us.

I was delighted that they had succeeded in crossing to the icefall; it was a step which I had rated as one of the hardest before us; but when we asked them how they had fared to-day they were non-committal; all they would say was, "We haven't got through it."

Back in the tents they told us their story. They had climbed the wall on which we first saw them, had overcome an over-hanging section by fixing a rope stirrup to a piton hammered into the ice above the overhang, and had then found themselves in a section very much broken, a jumble of blocks resembling, Band said, parts of the Khumbu Icefall. This section, which was fairly straightforward, ended against a vertical, sometimes overhanging, wall fifty feet high, which seemed to stretch across the whole breadth of the icefall. At first they had prospected to the right, where the wall was split from top to bottom by several cracks, and there might, they thought, be a way; but there was none; they found themselves in an ice-cavern whose sides towered up to meet above their heads. Then they looked to the left, where some hard and delicate ice-climbing led them to unstable ground near the right bank of the icefall, a dangerous route which seemed not to take them any nearer the top. When they turned for camp they had decided that there was nothing for it but the middle of the wall, where a flake of ice partly split from it offered a means of cutting steps for the first thirty feet.

Next day, Jackson and I went with them to see for ourselves. Band and Hardie led the way; Jackson and I followed.

The hundred-foot climb above the bergschrund was even less secure than it had looked. From the recess it was necessary to climb a few feet, and then to ease yourself gingerly to the right round a vertical corner on glassy ice, holding on to its flutings. Every now and then you knocked off a chip, which tinkled down into the waiting schrund, its mouth now fifty feet below. Round the corner the slope eased, but was still steep, about fifty degrees. Every thirty feet or so, where there was a block of solid ice, a piton was fixed, and we moved one at a time, using these pitons as belays. But mostly the ice was not fit to hold pitons. It was rotten, and honeycombed. We were never sure what the results of a blow with the axe would be; sometimes a block would come away when struck, sometimes the pick went through without effort into one of the holes with which the ice-mass was riddled. We had the feeling that we were trusting ourselves to a pile of blocks which at any moment might collapse.

At the top of this slope we followed the footsteps of the first pair to the top of the mass of ice which hung over the recess, and from there round another corner on our left, moving towards the middle of the icefall. It was an airy walk along a sloping gangway above a wall so steep that we could not, from above, see it. All we could see below was a great trough, about eighty feet down, strewn with ice which had broken from the wall on which we stood. Above us was an overhang. In fifty feet our ledge came to an end in a corner; here the wall above was still overhanging, but short, and a loop of rope dangled over its lip.

Grasping it, and digging my crampons into the ice below the overhang, I hauled myself onto the sloping ice above, where there was a piton. We enlarged the steps and cut away some of the lip of the overhang; but it was always a strenuous pull, which at this height, close to 20,000 feet, left us gasping. We were now in the 'Khumbu' section, and fifty yards farther on we saw Hardie and Band already at the foot of their wall.

They were cutting steps up the partly detached pillar of ice which here sloped up the wall from right to left for forty feet. By cutting steps in a very awkward position it would be possible to use the pillar to surmount the first overhanging twenty feet of the wall. Hardie was working on the pillar, safeguarded every few feet by his rope threaded through rings clipped to pitons driven into the ice above him. It was slow work, and for the next hour Jackson and I scouted round to the right, in case yesterday the others had missed some easier way; but they had not.

When we came back, Hardie had reached a point thirty feet up the pillar, where he cut a large step. Above this the

wall was only vertical, but the pillar, here beginning to be
detached, could no longer be used, and the only way seemed
to be to try the last twenty feet straight up, by what is known as
'artificial climbing'. Band took over, chipped a few nicks for
his feet, and, using his great reach, hammered in several pitons
above his head. He clipped his rope to a high piton, and while
Hardie hauled on it below, drew himself up, using other
pitons as handholds until he could hammer in one higher
still. We watched with our hearts in our mouths. His crampon
points had little hold on the ice, and sometimes he would, by a
slight variation of the direction of pull, easily lift out of the ice
a piton on which he had just been relying. Every pull had to
come in exactly the right direction or he would be off. At last
he could reach up to drive his axe into snow in a crevasse at
the top of the wall, and a moment later he was up. We let
out a cheer.

It was now one o'clock; we had been out for four hours, and
it was clear that we would not finish our exploration to-day
but must climb the wall again to-morrow; so Jackson and I
went back to camp for stakes and a rope ladder. As we turned to
climb down the lower overhanging pitch we saw Hardie join
Band at the top of the wall.

By three o'clock we were back at its foot. It was misty now,
and beginning to snow. Hardie and Band hauled up the stakes
and fixed the ladder, which hung down as far as the middle of
the pillar, its lower end free.

We were not happy that night. On the radio MacKinnon,
who had seen us that afternoon from the shoulder of Talung,
told us that we were taking the best line through the icefall:
"You have only three or four more wedding-cakes to pass."
But the route above the ladder had seemed bad to Hardie, and
he was not hopeful at all of reaching the top of the Lower
Icefall from there. Even below the ladder, I thought parts of
the route were not only difficult but conspicuously dangerous,

and already I doubted if there was justification for bringing Sherpas along it. The first slope above the bergschrund would never be safe, and it was only a matter of time before even the great upper wall climbed to-day collapsed with movement of the glacier and was strewn, a chaos of blocks, in the level section now beneath it. The only encouraging news was that Band and Hardie from above their wall had seen the upper part of the east face of the Western Buttress. The lower part of this face is impossibly steep, and the upper part, where it overlooks the Plateau, so formidable that so far we had seen no way of traversing it even if we could reach it from the west; but at the level of the top of the Lower Icefall, Band and Hardie had seen in it a snow-gully which ran down from the crest of the buttress to the top of the Lower Icefall, and they had thought it looked climbable. If we could not use the Lower Icefall route, or did not think it right to do so, there was now a possibility that we might reach the top of this gully by the west slope of the Western Buttress, come down the gully, by-pass nearly the whole of the Lower Icefall and still reach the Plateau. We had noticed this gully in photographs taken from Talung Peak and from the air, but in those pictures its angle was exaggerated, and we had not considered it as part of a possible way. To-morrow, we would have a final look at the Lower Icefall and, if we decided that it would not do, would put all our strength into an attempt from the other side to reach the top of this gully, the place that later came to be called the Hump.

We started early, and Jackson and I found the wall exciting enough even with a rope ladder. Above it, we wound among some large crevasses, as far as a prominent ice-nose, 'the dragon's mouth', a rotted, undercut obstacle. We climbed it straight, and after passing more crevasses reached an area which seemed recently to have subsided, a hollow in the glacier full of clean-cut blocks of all shapes and sizes. We crossed it one at a time, and climbed the slope beyond. It was an enjoyable slope, and at the top of it I cut up a short ice-wall. I found myself on the lip of a deep wide crevasse which stretched to right and left with no sign of a bridge. For to-day we were stopped. We were about four hundred feet above the top of Kempe's Buttress, and about as far below the Plateau.

We sat on the edge of the crevasse, speculating about the part of the icefall immediately ahead. Probably, with ladders, we could bridge this crevasse; but what about the next, and the one after? It did not much matter: I had already made up my mind that we could not use this route. We could not ask Sherpas to come this way, slowly, burdened, day after day. Casualties would not merely be likely, they would be certain.

We could now see more clearly the gully that came down from the Hump, and it looked good. We decided to put everything into an effort to reach the top of it from the far side, and we turned down to move our base to the foot of the slopes above Pache's Grave.

CHAPTER SIX

THE ROUTE OVER THE HUMP

April 23rd–April 28th

WE were back at Base at five, all rather tired, and all disappointed. Our choice of a route was narrowed, and the chance of success seemed more slender. We had now no time to waste if we were to explore the slopes above Pache's Grave and find a way over the Hump in time to put camps high on the mountain.

Hardie and Band thought that the finding of a way to the Plateau was their particular task, and wanted to finish it; and on April 23rd they and I went over to have a first look at the new line.

We cut north across the broken glacier between our camp and the right bank of the Yalung, aiming for the foot of the Western Buttress, and then following the right bank down, skirting the foot of that buttress in a stony trough between the glacier and the rocks. In an hour and a half a wide rocky gully took us north again round the nose of the buttress to the edge of the glacier on its west flank, and we found ourselves on a level with the knoll on which Pache had been buried. It was a rounded hump, covered with boulders and earth. Under the thin layer of fresh snow there was moss and grass, and we found here traces of the first expedition to Kangchenjunga: rusty tins, a couple of stone shelter-walls, and Pache's grave, a wooden cross and a stone carved, "Alexis A Pache. 1. ix. 1905." Looking north-east, we saw on the right the steep edge, sometimes snow, sometimes rock, of the Western Buttress; straight ahead were the lower slopes of the glaciated mountain-side

The Yalung face from the air

which fell for seven thousand feet from the west ridge of Kang-chenjunga West. Two thousand feet above us, before rising again towards this ridge, the edge of the Western Buttress flattened out; and we guessed that there was the top of the Hump. The way to it did not seem impossible. Below it, the west face of the buttress was shaped like an hour-glass: its upper slopes, of snow, were broad at the top, and led down to a funnel-like passage, flanked on each side by ice-cliffs. Below the narrows the snow-slopes broadened again, becoming part of the glacier which flowed down past us, towards our left, to join the main Yalung below Pache's Grave; the steep side of this glacier, a hundred yards away, could be reached easily. Only two places seemed dangerous: the lower snow-field, which was threatened by ice from a small but very unstable-looking ice-cliff south of the narrows, and the narrows themselves, which might be a funnel receiving any snow or ice falling from the upper part of the slope. We thought we might put Camp 1 above the narrows, protected from such falls by a crevasse. It did not look a safe route, but it was much safer than the Lower Icefall, and we settled that to-morrow Hardie and Band should come up with two Sherpas, find a place for Camp 1, and next day try to reach the Hump to see what lay on the other side of it.

In the meantime we wanted a site for a base camp here, and the knoll of Pache's Grave seemed a good one. Its earth and sparse vegetation would be a great improvement on our present base camp. There, there was only ice and stones. Moreover, although we thought it safe from avalanche, we could not be certain that it was so. Only a few days earlier, Hardie and Band had been startled there by a huge avalanche from Talung Peak, when thousands of tons of ice had crashed down the Cresta Run, and the camp had been enveloped in a great cloud of ice-dust which spread across the whole valley. When all was over, it was as though there had been a heavy snowfall: the camp was covered in ice-dust several inches deep. There, too, we were camped on a glacier, and disturbed often by the sudden cracking of the ice—'zong'. That very morning the Sherpas had taken me to see a crevasse two or three inches wide which had suddenly appeared running across the floor of the cook-house, and during the past days we had noticed many smaller cracks appearing for the first time not far from our tents. This new site would not only be right on our route, it would be more comfortable and more cheerful; and we decided to move over at once. In the course of the next ten days we brought there from Corner and from our old base the stores to be used in the weeks to come.

Before turning back on the 23rd, we went on to the beginning of the Hump route. The edge of the glacier was two hundred feet high, steep dry ice, and we cut steps up it, and for an hour broke trail in deep snow in the direction of the narrows until we were clear of crevasses and the route to the narrows lay straight before us. Here and there around us were old blocks fallen from the ice-cliff which threatened this part of the route; as far as possible, we chose a route which skirted below them, and which sidled for shelter under small walls of ice.

It was the day on which Mather and MacKinnon were attempting Talung Peak. We had heard this by radio the night before, and had all the time been on the look-out for them. When we picked them out they were above the line of huge seracs that bars the way to the upper snow-fields of the mountain; it looked as if they had climbed the serac wall at its west end, its steepest part, and as if nothing now lay between them and the top but steep unbroken snow. It was, however, late in the day before they had found their way through, and they were forced to come down. Before the weather allowed of another attempt, we were too deeply engaged on Kangchenjunga itself to go again, and Talung Peak is still unclimbed.

The main traffic from Corner was still going to our old base;

59

on the way back, therefore, we cut straight across the glacier, and joined the route from Corner to Base near the first boulder, the roping-up place. Next morning Brown and I came down from the old base in time to intercept that day's carry and direct it to Pache's Grave.

Meanwhile Hardie and Band had taken two Sherpas to pitch camp in the narrows, or above, but had been unable, because of mist, to find a safe site. They had made a dump, and come back to the new base.

We had six inches of snow that night, and it was still snowing and overcast when I woke. From the old base I spoke to the other camps on the radio, and found that conditions were the same there; we were all waiting. But the forecast to-day was fair; at eleven it was fine enough to start, and the old base was abandoned for good.

On the 26th it was fine. Hardie and Band started for Camp 1, and Brown went with them so that he should know the way there. The plan was that as soon as Hardie and Band had found a way over the Hump, Brown and I should go over and live at Camp 2 on the Plateau to prospect above, while stores were ferried over the Hump by the rest of the expedition.

When Brown and I started up on the morning of the 27th, it was misty and we could see nothing of Hardie and Band; but we could hear them, over a thousand feet higher, working on the ice above Camp 1, and every now and then a long 'Coo-ee' or 'O Lama O' came floating down to us. We started at eight-thirty, and were on the glacier at nine. From its edge, it took one and a quarter hours of hard drudgery to reach their camp. We could see nothing; the debris in the snow reminded us of the ice-cliff above, but the monotonous labour of putting one foot before the other deadened all feeling of danger. It was hot and muggy, and the last pull up to the camp was steep.

The camp was pitched in a crevasse choked with snow. It was level with the middle of the narrows, rather to the right as

Lower Icefall

Left Jackson and Band crossing from Kempe's Buttress
Right Band on the fifty-foot wall

we came up; to our left was the deepest part of the narrows down which any ordinary avalanche would go, and beyond this trough was a region of great walls and crevasses which stretched as far as we could see. Above us, a big crevasse cut right across the slope, and seemed to give good protection to the camp; but we wondered how and where Hardie and Band had managed to cross it. Cross it they had, because earlier, through a break in cloud, we had seen them going strongly up the slopes towards the Hump.

After a rest we followed their tracks to find out. Above camp, they had gone to the left along a blade of snow, and climbed down to reach the floor of the narrows. Stepping over a crevasse they had gone for a hundred feet straight up a steep slope to the lower lip of the big crevasse. Its walls here were vertical, and the lip to which we looked across about twenty feet higher than that on which we stood. To the right we could see no bridge; to the left the crevasse disappeared under ice-cliffs hundreds of feet high. At first we could not see which way they had gone. Then we saw their track on the far wall of the crevasse, thirty feet away. This wall, vertical opposite us, and overhung by ice-cliffs, farther to the right led to a snow-slope at forty-five degrees, up which their track continued. From where we stood, they had gone a few yards to the left, and crossed a snow-bridge which ended against the far wall of the crevasse. From the far side of the bridge they had cut a ledge across the wall from left to right, rising slightly to gain the foot of the snow-slope. We followed. The snow-bridge, though it seemed thick, sagged in the middle, and the ice on the traverse, when we reached it, was brittle, breaking away in chunks when we struck it. Under the ledge the ice-cliff was tucked in, and the only thing to be seen below us was the shadowed green-blue depth of the crevasse. We edged along for fifteen feet, pushed outwards by the bulging ice above the ledge, until we were able to round a corner and drive our axe-shafts into

61

16 Base Camp 2   Looking south towards Corner Camp

the snow of the slope above. This was less steep, but the snow was of poor quality: the upper layer was rather soft, though that beneath was firmer. After two hundred feet, the angle eased and the quality of the snow improved; we moved together, and climbed steadily in mist looking for some sign of the Hump. Half-way there, Band and Hardie appeared coming down; they shouted that they had crossed the Hump, had climbed the top part of the Lower Icefall and had found a way to the Plateau.

We came down and spent the afternoon at Camp 1 digging caves in the snow. There was little room for tents, and two good caves would have been useful; unfortunately, after digging a foot, we came to ice, and although we persevered, and at last had two small caves at this camp, they were hardly worth the effort it cost to make them.

Though we were pleased to know that we had a route by-passing nearly the whole of the Lower Icefall, it was a pleasure tempered by two things, the realization that much had to be done to the track over the great crevasse before it could be a porter's highway, and the fear that we might soon be running the risk of avalanche on the slopes above the crevasse. These great expanses of snow below the Hump were a cause of anxiety. They were steep; the snow lay thick on them; they were convex; and they faced the afternoon sun. It was a pity to have to plan a route that went so soon over such slopes, slopes that with any sudden warmth, or a fall of new snow, might quickly become impassable, and entrap, as was within a few days to happen, a party that was above them.

We had, however, no alternative but that of giving up the expedition; and we had one thing to be thankful for, that in our fear here of avalanche we were concerned not with the caprice of ice, but with snow, whose behaviour we could to some extent predict. We determined early to make our journeys over the Hump as far as possible before the sun had softened this snow, to treat it carefully after any new fall, and to be off the mountain before the temperature rose at the approach of the monsoon; this last was the greatest danger; once softened by the monsoon, the snow would in all likelihood stay soft.

The ascent from Camp 1 to Camp 2 could be very pleasant. The convex slopes swept unbroken from the crests above and to the north of us down towards the funnel of the narrows, and as they vanished below gave a sense of airiness. In the early morning, when they were hard, they were a delight to climb; the air was frosty, the sun when it reached us bright, and the snow sparkled. But early starts were never easy from Camp 1. It was in shadow until eight o'clock; and although on the day on which we first occupied Camp 2 it was at five that we began to prepare to start, we did not leave camp till eight, nor cross the big crevasse till nine-thirty.

At the top of the Hump there was a saddle fifty yards across. Near its far side, running parallel with the line of the ridge of the Hump, was a crevasse, the far wall of which was a decaying fringe of ice-pinnacles that cut off the view. Band and Hardie led the way to where the crevasse was narrow enough to jump across, and up a fifteen-foot chimney in the ice beyond. We sidled along an ice-ledge under one of the pinnacles, and reached a gap.

The snow-gully we had seen from the Lower Icefall was at our feet; it was steep, and fell for five hundred feet to that icefall. To our left were towers and walls of rock falling to the Plateau. To our right were the cliffs of ice and rock overlooking the Lower Icefall. Straight ahead, across the top of the Lower Icefall, we saw the Upper Icefall. It came down for three thousand feet from the edge of the Great Shelf. Between it and Kangchenjunga West, to the left as we looked, was the broad Valley, at the head of which, and overhanging it, were ice-cliffs which bordered the Great Shelf. The floor of the Valley also was broken in places into ice-cliffs, and ice-cliffs hung high above it on the face of Kangchenjunga West. Its lower end flattened out, joining the ice flowing from the Upper Icefall to form the nearly level Plateau. The Upper Icefall itself, which we had feared might in places be swept by avalanches from near the head of the Valley, now seemed like a broad, blunt ridge, its north slope broken and forming one wall of the Valley, its crest rounded, and also broken in places, particularly towards the top, by cliffs of ice, and its south slope very steep, plunging abruptly down towards the easternmost of the gullies between Kempe's Buttress and the cliffs under the Great Shelf. Surely, if we could find a route winding up among those ice-cliffs on the crest of the Upper Icefall, we should have a safe way to the Great Shelf.

The gully down to the Lower Icefall was easy to descend; the snow was still firm. The gully ran into the icefall three hundred feet below its top. Between the two there was a crevasse, which we crossed at first by a snow-bridge, later by a ladder. Here the icefall itself was comparatively easy to walk through, but the going was laborious. The place was airless, a sun-trap from whose walls the light and heat were reflected fiercely. Though there was no technical difficulty until the final ice-wall at the top of the icefall, this was always a tedious section of the route, more tiring and depressing than many a steeper pull on small ice-steps. To add to discomfort, we were on this day enveloped here in thin cloud, and when at last we reached the wall at the top of the icefall, we were going very slowly. Band and Hardie had climbed this wall the previous evening by cutting steps up the edge of a partly detached flake, shaped like the prow of an old-fashioned battleship. We went the same way, and found it a hard pull. The loads were hauled up one by one, and we plodded, now in thick cloud, through soft snow, looking for a place to camp. Snow was falling when at last, about two hundred yards above the wall, we swung off our loads, sinking them into the snow and subsiding on them ourselves for a rest before putting up the tent. We could only see about twenty yards. Suddenly, somewhere above us, there was a rumbling noise which rapidly swelled to a thunderous roar. We could see nothing, and anxiously waited to know where the avalanche was going. The noise subsided; still we could see nothing; we relaxed. A few minutes later a second avalanche came down; still we saw nothing; no snow fell; no blast blew by. When the third and the fourth avalanches had fallen, still without coming near, it seemed to us that our proposed camp-site must be fairly safe, and we put up the tent. We found later that these avalanches were from a hanging glacier far up on the west ridge of Kangchenjunga West. They fell into the upper part of the Plateau, but were never large enough to travel down it through the soft snow to our camp.

When the tent was pitched, Hardie, Band and the Sherpas started down, leaving us to the mist and the solitude.

CHAPTER SEVEN

THE UPPER ICEFALL

April 29th – May 8th

WE were now about one hundred feet lower than the top of the Hump, at a height, according to Hardie's surveys, of about 20,400 feet. While Hardie saw to the improvement of the route over the Hump, and set in motion a daily lift of stores to Camp 2, Brown and I planned to explore as far as our future Camp 3.

We discovered in the morning that we were near the lower end of a gently sloping glacier, not much crevassed. It was not a very good morning; there was mist and sunshine in turn, all the tops were covered with filmy cloud, and there had been six inches of snow in the night; but we saw enough to plan ahead. Our glacier, the Plateau, was about a quarter of a mile wide and half a mile long. Looking up it to the north we saw on the left the cliffs of the ridge whose lower part is the Hump; straight ahead was the south face of Kangchenjunga West, an unbroken precipice seven thousand feet high, of rock and fluted ice; on the right was the Upper Icefall. Except for the occasional contribution of an ice-avalanche from high on the face of Kangchenjunga West, our level glacier was formed from the Upper Icefall, and from the Valley, the ice-filled depression north of it, into which fell any avalanches that came from the rickety ice-cliffs at the edge of the part of the Great Shelf nearest Kangchenjunga West. We had never been able, either from air-photographs or from the photographs of the expedition of 1954, to form a clear idea of the form of this Plateau, or to decide on its degree of safety from avalanche. Now that

66

we were on it, it was smaller than we had expected, and easier to cross; moreover, it seemed safe. We crossed it in a straight line, heading for a promising snow-slope between two ice-cliffs at the middle of the foot of the Upper Icefall. The snow was soft and deep on the flat, and soft, too, in many places on the icefall, though in other places there we found bare snow-ice, where the overlying soft snow had slipped away. On April 29th we made steady progress, plodding through the soft snow and cutting in the snow-ice, and by twelve-thirty were near 22,000 feet, two or three hundred feet below where we were later to place Camp 3. By this time we were very tired, and it was cold, misty, and beginning to snow; we sat to rest on the lower lip of a crevasse, the only kind of place on this slope where it was possible to sit without cutting a seat. When we started in the morning our sack had seemed light enough. There was not much in it: a few pitons, a hammer and a tin of peaches. We had carried it in turns, and each time I had picked it up it had seemed twice as heavy as last time; by now it weighed a ton. We cached the pitons and hammer, leaving the peaches, too, after finding them solid ice, and started down. We were tired out when we reached our tent, but we knew that next time we should go up more quickly and with less fatigue.

That night we heard on the radio that a depression was centred over Kangchenjunga and that the weather was expected to deteriorate. Two feet of snow fell in the night, and in the morning the tent was half buried. Walking outside was difficult; we sank over our knees; but we had with us fuel for only one day more, and in view of the forecast we decided that we must try to come down while we could. Ordinarily it took half an hour from Camp 2 to reach the top of the Hump; this day it took two hours and a half. In the Lower Icefall there was no sign of our tracks of yesterday, and we struggled in the deep snow through a tangle of blocks, often falling with

67

a leg through a hole of unknown depth. At the foot of the gully leading to the Hump we found the spill of a small avalanche, and the snow was up to our thighs. At first we could make no headway at all, slipping back at every effort as far as we heaved ourselves upward. Then Brown tried ploughing on all fours, while I followed in the furrow. Here in half an hour we gained sixty feet. As we toiled through the drift there was a hissing sound, and from a gully in the rocks on our right a small avalanche of new snow poured past us and over us into the bergschrund behind. Long before we reached the top of the slope, to make each step was a deliberate act of will. Thankfully we climbed down the ice-chimney, stepped over the crevasse to the flat saddle of the Hump, and dragged ourselves over to look at the slopes going down to Camp 1. We did not like the look of them, but thought that we should at least try them. We went very cautiously for a hundred feet, Brown in front; the snow seemed to pack fairly well under us, but it was heavy and incoherent, in places thigh-deep. We had not yet come to the place where the convex slope grew steep.

Suddenly Brown stopped: "Did you hear that?" I took a step forward in front of him, to feel the snow myself, and at my step the sound he had heard was repeated, but louder, a quiet 'hrumph' somewhere under us, and a crack opened in the snow at my feet, running across the slope. We waited, axe-shafts deep in snow that was too soft to be secure, not daring to move. Then very carefully, and as fast as we could, we retraced our steps to the Hump. The prospect was not cheerful: our battle had been lost, and we might now be cut off for days. But to persist in going down would have been suicide, and there was nothing for it but to face the return to Camp 2. When at last we reached our tent, it was, as I put in my diary that night, 'with much labour'. We were taking ten steps on the level glacier, then sitting in the snow to rest; taking ten more, and resting again. We lay in our bags until evening.

68

17 Above Camp 1

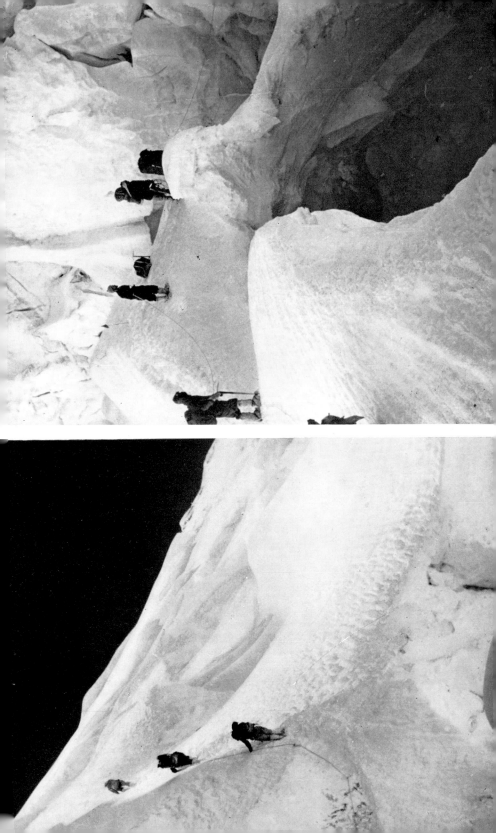

18 The crest of the Hump   Looking to the Upper Icef

The Hump gully   Looking down to the upper part of the Lower Icefall

When I spoke to Base Camp on the radio, they told us that Hardie and Clegg had tried to-day to come up to us with supplies, but that on the slope above Camp 1 they had started an avalanche; luckily it was not a big one, but it was enough to warn them to turn back. We wondered how long it would be before the new snow would be safe to cross. Much would depend on the weather, but I thought the slope unlikely to be safe in less than two days, and told those at Base to take no chances with it.

The morning was brilliantly fine, but Brown and I did not stir: the snow was everywhere deep, and we were still weary. We spoke to Base and discouraged any attempt to cross the Hump to-day. Clouds gathered, and by noon were thick about us. We had settled down for the afternoon, at intervals melting snow for drinks, when we heard a faint shout. We shouted back, and crawled from the tent; there was nothing to be seen in the mist. I began to clear a site for a second tent, and Brown put more snow on the stove. Another call came from below, more urgent, "What about a hand?" We picked up the rope and went to meet them: Hardie, Streather and several Sherpas. They had brought up a rope ladder and fixed it to the wall alongside the battleship bow, but to climb it was hard work, and some of the Sherpas were in difficulties. All the party were on the verge of exhaustion when they reached the tents; it had been a tough struggle; but Hardie thought that the west slopes of the Hump were now reasonably safe. They had brought us a good supply of fuel and food, and an end to our isolation.

When they went down they left us two Sherpas, Kunde Ang Dawa and Aila, who set up their tent in line with ours, joining the two sleeve-entrances to make one room. They moved our Lilos, levelled the tent floor, and cleared away the accumulated garbage of three days, wiping up a mess of powdered milk that had collected under us. When they had taken into their own tent the apparatus of cooking, we could lie at

69

20 The bergschrund between the Hump gully and the Lower Icefall

full length. It was snowing again, but now I did not care. The patter of the wind-driven flakes mingled with the murmur of Sherpa voices. The cold edge of outer space had been changed into a part of the world of every day.

There were six more inches of snow in the night, but it was fine on the morning of May 2nd, and three of us started for the Upper Icefall; Aila waited in camp, since Band and Mac-Kinnon were expected over the Hump from Camp 1, MacKinnon to stay with us.

We followed the old route, and reached our previous highest point in half an hour less than on the first occasion. It was the beginning of an improvement in the route which continued steadily, the hardening of the track underfoot. The first journey through to Camp 3, two days later, took six hours; six days after that, on May 10th, Hardie and I went up in one hour fifty minutes, and by May 18th the ordinary daily run there by laden porters took under two hours. The distance was half a mile on the level, followed by a climb of fourteen hundred feet. We left Ang Dawa to rest where we had cached the pitons on our earlier visit, and tackled the band of ice-cliffs above. First we went towards the left, but after climbing an unstable ice-wall we found progress stopped by a series of crevasses over which there were no natural bridges. We tried again farther to the right, and climbed another wall, only to find, again, a crevasse which we could not cross. There was a third possible way, up a gully in the ice-cliffs still farther to the right, but we were now too tired to try it, and we put it off until next day.

The afternoon was well advanced, the valley was full of heavy black clouds, there was a strong wind, and it had begun to snow. We had barely started down before the storm was on us: the wind swept fiercely across the exposed slopes, driving snow before it, filling every step we had cut on the way up, and forcing us to bend over our axes, and shield our faces with our hands. The flags we had planted on the way up were invisible until we were close upon them. We had to feel our way down, by memory of the direction of each flag from the last. I was ahead, Ang Dawa, very tired, in the middle; Brown safeguarded us from behind, and helped to keep us on our course when one flag was lost to sight and the next not yet found. At last we were down on the level ice-field, where our old track showed faintly.

At camp we found MacKinnon. He had come, but no more tents, so we crammed for the night into one two-man tent. Mackinnon had brought up the latest batch of letters, and Brown and I slipped into our bags to read them, leaving him to cope with the problem of finding a way into his own bag, between ours. For a long time we watched him lying with one leg in and one out, panting, too tired in the cramped space to make the next move.

It snowed all night, and was snowing next morning, so once again we stayed in. At one o'clock Streather appeared from below, bringing a lift of stores. No weather seemed to stop these lifts from Base, by Camp 1, to Camp 2. From the day when Hardie and Streather had forced a way through to relieve Brown and me, not a day's lift was missed for over three weeks. Each afternoon six or eight escorted Sherpas would leave Base for Camp 1. They slept there, some in tents, some in a cave. Next morning they carried over the Hump to Camp 2 and returned unladen to Base. Starts from Camp 1 were early as a matter of policy, and often the lift would reach Camp 2 before the party there had started for Camp 3. Soon after midday they would be back at Base Camp, ready to start up again twenty-four hours later. They were escorted by Dawa Tenzing, and by those of the climbing party who were at Base for the time being. We took turns; and some of us, because it seemed less enervating to sleep at Camp 1 than at Base, stayed up there to make trips over the Hump on two or three successive days.

At last, on May 4th, we reached the site for Camp 3, and found a way to the upper part of the Upper Icefall. We all went: Brown, MacKinnon and Ang Dawa were on the first rope, Aila and I followed. The Sherpas were loaded with hemp rope, Dural angle-iron stakes, and pitons; I had a four-pound iron mallet with which to drive in the stakes.

We fixed two hundred feet of rope on a steep slope at the foot of the icefall, and more on a long slope of snow-ice farther up. Each time we had come up we had had to re-cut our zig-zag of steps. To-day, MacKinnon cut huge steps straight up in one line. It was slow work. We moved up a step, then waited a few minutes while MacKinnon cut the next; sometimes Aila and I would wait until several had been cut, and then move up five or six steps without stopping. It was a pleasant way to spend a morning, secure in big steps of snow-ice, the slope sweeping away below us, the great ice-walls of Kangchenjunga West towering above. Around us a steady stream of ice-chips from MacKinnon's axe tinkled down.

Half-way up the slope I stopped and drove in my axe to anchor myself, took one of the Dural stakes out of Aila's sack and banged it into the slope. It went in with a satisfying firmness, the snow-ice gripping it tighter at each stroke of the hammer. At the top of the slope we drove in two more, and hung four hundred feet of hemp rope down.

The angle now eased as far as the foot of the ice-cliffs which had stopped us two days earlier. We made straight for the gully that we had so far left unexplored, leaving the two Sherpas to rest on the ledge below the cliffs. The floor of the gully was full of loose powder snow which slipped away as Brown stepped into it. He cut steps instead up the wall on his right, and then, thirty feet up, where the snow was firmer, across the bed of the gully to the left. Here there was a ridge of ice, a few steps in which brought us to level ground above the lowest ice-cliff, but below the largest of all, a cliff sixty feet high which stretched

72

the whole breadth of the face. We had suspected, from the air-photographs and from the views we had had of the Upper Icefall from the top of the Hump, that we might by-pass this cliff by going left, yet without entering the avalanche-swept Valley. Now we went to see, hoping, too, that if we by-passed the cliff we might find above it a good camp-site. The foot of the cliff, and the ledge running along it, rose gently towards the left. We followed it, turning a couple of blind corners, and finding the ledge still there. Half-way along, at what was later the site of Camp 3, there was a break. The ledge here was ten feet wide, but we had to cross a crevasse and climb a twenty-foot ice-slope to reach its continuation. We pushed on. The ledge dwindled to nothing, the slope here dropping straight from the foot of the cliff at an angle of about thirty degrees. The snow lay loose on ice, and we moved one at a time, safe-guarding each other with ice-axe belays. Two hundred feet beyond the future site of Camp 3 the ice-cliff came to an end. I took a few steps up the slope beyond it, and saw our way clear ahead for several hundred feet over ice and snow. It was steep, thirty to forty degrees, and bare; it did not promise a good tent-site; but as far as we could see there was no obstacle to movement. We went a little higher, slowly now, in soft snow, but still we could see nowhere fit for the fairly large camp that we wanted to pitch here. There was no shelter, either from weather, or from slides of surface snow. We decided to sacrifice a little height and put our camp under the main ice-cliff, where the ledge was at its broadest; the height of the place we later calculated to be 21,800 feet. It was three-fifteen when we started down, and four-thirty when we reached camp. It had been a long day, eight hours of steady going, but we were jubilant: we had a sound site for Camp 3, and a route through the big seracs half-way up the Upper Icefall.

The next thing was to set up Camp 3, to stock it, and to have a daily lift there from Camp 2 while the lift to Camp 2 from

Base continued. Before going above Camp 3, I wanted it so well stocked that, if necessary, a dozen men could live there for two weeks. We planned now that MacKinnon and Neil Mather, who was to come up next day, should be in charge of the lift up to Camp 3 with six Sherpas under Annullu. Twelve other Sherpas would be living at Base and working over the Hump, six loads coming up each day. We had in all twenty-six Sherpas equipped to go at least as high as Camp 3; and although one or two were always out of action through fatigue or sickness, we were on the whole successful in keeping these numbers at these tasks.

Now that the lifts to Camps 2 and 3 would to-morrow be in full swing, the next aim ought to be a quick, long-range exploration to the top of the Great Shelf; and I went down to Base to discuss it with Hardie.

The Hump route was already transformed. At the battleship bow a metal ladder had replaced the rope ladder; instead of the awkward ice-pitches on top of the Hump, another metal ladder spanned the crevasse there; the track down was a trodden highway, and the passage of the traverse and the big crevasse above Camp 1 were now simple, at least for a party coming down unladen. It took us only an hour to reach Camp 1. We had time to look round at the steep curving fields of untouched snow; every hundred yards a route-flag made a splash of colour; below, after days on snow, the boulder-strewn reaches of the Yalung glacier by Corner Camp looked unreal; there were clouds between us and Jannu, and the light in the valley was always changing.

74

CHAPTER EIGHT

LIFE ON THE MOUNTAIN
AND AT BASE

TILL the time came for the final climbs, we used, in a general way, to take turns at going to the highest of the camps, and at coming to Base for a rest.

To some extent the body can adapt itself to a lack of oxygen: this is what the mountaineer calls acclimatization; and he naturally wants to benefit by it as much as he can. But lack of oxygen reaches at great heights a degree with which the body cannot, for long, cope: acclimatization may perhaps continue, but strength begins to drain away; I believe that to live for more than a few days at much over 22,000 feet, without rests at lower camps, generally does more harm than good.

Nor was lack of oxygen the only trial at high camps. There was the heat and glare of the tropical sun, and at night a cold that was like the malice of a living enemy. There was no greenery, no life, not even, at hand, rock to touch: nothing but ice and snow.

All the high camps were on ice and snow; and at all, movement was confined, either by the steepness around them or, if the place were relatively level, by a depth of soft snow that made walking a labour. Camp 1 was set on a kind of balcony looking across to Jannu; from it there was only a short easy journey down to Base. At any camp above, there was always a slight feeling of being cut off: even when there was little danger of avalanche on the slope west of the Hump, there was always, for men going down, the soft snow of the five-hundred-foot gully east of it to be climbed, uphill. Camp 2, in the great

75

cwm of the Plateau, was the best sheltered. Over the others there was generally a strong wind blowing, driving the snow. The annoyance of wind-driven snow was greatest where, as at Camp 3, there were cliffs of ice above: there, snow was lifted from the ledges and carried down swirling onto the tents, so that work outside them was particularly troublesome.

In calm sunny weather it was not unusual to climb at over 20,000 feet in shirt-sleeves, and at Camp 3, at 22,000 feet, the temperature by day in the shade could be so high that it was possible to lie in a tent stripped to the waist and still be uncomfortably hot. But a few hours later, at night, the thermometer might read zero, and breath be condensing in snowflakes on the walls of the tent and on the sleeping-bags. Inside the tent, as a rule, clothing was a string vest, thick woollen shirt and pants, a sweater, and light windproof trousers; when cloud hid the sun, and at morning and evening, it was necessary to add a jacket, and sometimes trousers, of eiderdown; to go outside, unless it was still, a man needed also a windproof smock. On his feet were woollen socks, never taken off, and over them, in the sleeping-bag, eiderdown socks; over these again, to go out of the tent, he wore either fur-lined boots or soft-soled canvas covers that came to the knees. At the lower camps it was pleasant to sleep in two bags clad only in woollen pants and shirt; but at the highest camps there was generally only one bag for each man, and at night the eiderdown suit was worn in it. Under the bag always was the air-mattress, the Lilo.

The food for the high camps had been chosen with care; but no care in the choice of food can, at those heights, create an appetite. Eating was difficult; there was little desire for anything but drink. Nausea was worst in the mornings: porridge, easily made, was often chosen for breakfast, but not many people, above Camp 3, were able to finish a plateful of it; usually a few spoonfuls were enough to drive a man from the tent to be rid of what he had swallowed. At evening, as a rule,

Below Camp 2   The rope ladder at the top of the Lower Icefall

22 Camp 2

Looking back to the Hu

things were better, and it was generally possible to stomach a mug of soup and some biscuits, with a little dried or tinned meat.

Above 23,000 feet the climber quickly loses weight and grows weak. He is like a sick man, always tired. To turn over in bed, to reach for a boot or a box of matches, brings an attack of breathlessness; every little exertion calls for an effort of will. For most of the time he is cramped in a small tent, and preoccupied with some personal discomfort: a sore throat, a persistent cough, a raw burn from the sun. It is only now and then that he wakes to the grandeur of the scene, or has for a fleeting moment a sense of the unfathomable strangeness of which it is a part. As vigour flags, interest is dulled, and it is not long before he begins to feel that he is making no progress in what he has undertaken and that he wishes he could be quit of it. To someone who had never known the power of the desire to climb a mountain—to set foot on it, to feel it with the hands, to be familiar with it in detail, to look at the world from it—life above 23,000 feet would seem strange. Could such a visitor have come to one of the high camps on Kangchenjunga and seen its listless occupants, he might well have wondered what had brought them there from so far.

At Base the tents were among boulders, on earth, where there was moss and some grass. They were roomy, a large Dome and some four-man Meades. Everyone could make his bed after a fashion his home, the space around filled with his belongings: a kit-bag of spare clothes, a wooden box on which to put books and writing-materials. For breakfast and lunch a table was set outside, where there was a view of the way to the Hump, and of anybody moving on it, up or down.

There was some local food. The quarters of a yak slaughtered at Moraine had been brought, and stored in a crevasse; and there were potatoes, eggs and rice. Appetites revived, thanks largely to Thondup, the cook. Thondup is an old hand, who has had many years of experience as cook to expeditions, and has the knack of turning any makeshift bivouac into a centre of comfort. As the party moved forward, he followed with his retinue, ten or a dozen coolies carrying cooking-gear and tarpaulins and long poles; and at each new base he set up his solid, weather-proof kitchen. Morning and afternoon would find one or other of us sitting before the fire, eating freshly made pancakes, stodgy perhaps by other standards, but delicious to a mouth weary of a diet of biscuits. As a place of relaxation the kitchen had only one drawback, the wood-smoke. Sherpa eyes are inured to it, and if Thondup tired of his visitors, he could drive them out by heaping his fire with damp juniper.

On the mountain, of course, the climber lived in his clothes. At Base, not only could he change; he could have a hot bath in the open, picking a sunny interval when the wind had dropped, usually at mid-morning, before the coming of the afternoon cloud. At Base, too, the glare of the snow could be forgotten, and goggles and face-cream be discarded.

Base was in close touch with the human world. Every night there was the weather-forecast from India, news and music from Ceylon. Sometimes there was the short-wave programme of the B.B.C. Once the sound of a referee's whistle was heard, blown at a cup-final at Wembley.

The track down the glacier was in sight all the way to Corner, and as the day drew near when the mail was expected everyone kept a look-out. Someone would see figures approaching, and all would gather to watch; then, when they were still too far to be recognized by ordinary eyes even through glasses, the Sherpas would say that it was only so-and-so, naming two of the coolies who brought wood for Thondup's fire. When at last the mail arrived, it often did so unannounced. During the evening meal in the Dome, Dawa Tenzing's head would appear through the door, as he passed in the canvas bag. The

78

runners, in darkness, had walked quietly into camp a few minutes before.

At Base there was also the company of other inhabitants. How they came there was a puzzle. These were the small rodents that the Sherpas call 'teiokpe'; the food, they say, of the 'yeti'. Grey-brown, with no tails, they look rather like guinea-pigs. An idle man could watch a burrow till one of them stole out, and see it nibble grass and twitch its nose till scared by an unguarded movement, when it would dart away a few feet before beginning to nibble again. John Clegg wanted to take one of the little beasts home preserved for dissection; but when at last one was caught for him, after a few minutes he let it go.

A stay at Base was a rest-cure. Two or three nights there renewed the desire to be on the mountain.

CHAPTER NINE

THE GREAT SHELF

May 9th–May 14th

FOR the exploration to Camp 5, I decided to use the two closed-circuit oxygen sets that we had with us.

When we had planned the expedition in England, we had determined to rely on the well proven open-circuit sets; but since Everest the closed-circuit sets had been modified in the light of Everest experience, and I had agreed to take to Kangchenjunga two closed-circuit sets for experiment. To test them it was necessary to have them in use on two or more consecutive days, by men experienced in their working, who would also during the test sleep with oxygen; and this ought to be done at a height where, if they went wrong, the consequences to the users would not be serious. Because there is no question that a closed-circuit set which is in working order enables the climber to move fast, this seemed the ideal opportunity for the trial. Norman Hardie, who was in charge of the sets and was familiar with them, and I, who had used them before, would start with them from Camp 3, find a way, if we could, to the Shelf, and there prospect for a site for a camp above the Shelf and for the start of a route to the final ridge.

We set off as soon as Camp 3 was stocked, on May 9th, and, after a night each at Camps 1 and 2, went up with Streather and Mather to Camp 3. During the week either Brown and MacKinnon, or Mather and Streather, had been coming up each day with half a dozen loads from Camp 2. Tents had been pitched on the shelf under the great ice-cliff here, and a cave had been dug at the foot of the cliff itself. This had taken a

week to dig; every day, after completing the carry, the Sherpas
had taken turns at enlarging it, hacking it out of solid ice chip
by chip with an ice-axe, and then shovelling out the chips; it
was now big enough to hold five Sherpas comfortably. When
we arrived on May 11th Mather and the Sherpas continued the
work on the cave, while Hardie collected all the oxygen
cylinders which had been brought up already and stacked them
on ledges cut out of the snow a few feet above camp. Meanwhile
Streather and I went above camp to fix a rope as a hand-rail
where our route traversed to the left to go round the north
end of the great ice-cliff.

Finally Mather and Streather went down, and Hardie and I
were left with two of our strongest Sherpas, Annullu and
Urkien. We were well, and hungry, a great contrast to the
exhaustion that Brown and I had felt on our first visit to this
height two weeks earlier. The camp faced west, and had no
sun until mid-morning; but in the afternoon, if it was clear,
the place was a sun-trap, and on this first afternoon I lay in
the tent on my sleeping-bag stripped to the waist. We were
now, if our exploration was successful, within a few days of an
attempt on the summit ridge, and as I lay I worked out what
would be wanted at each camp, how many men would be
needed to take it there, and what they would need at the camp
below. Hardie was outside preparing our oxygen sets for the
morrow, and when he had finished he came in and went over
the calculated quantities with me. If all went as we hoped,
when we came down in two days' time it would be to launch
the final moves.

Though Camp 3 was hot enough in the afternoons, in the
mornings it was bitterly cold. At nearly 22,000 feet, it was exposed to the west, and every morning there we were lashed by
a wind which swept masses of powder snow down from the
slopes above, and blew it into every corner. We found for
the first time on May 12th how difficult it was there to make an

early start. We fumbled with camp gear, packing tents and ropes and putting together our oxygen sets, constantly frustrated by the violent gusts which blew about camp the stinging clouds of snow. Snow covered the work on which we were engaged, stuck to all the metal and to the hands, and sifted down the back of the neck. We left at last at eight o'clock.

Hardie and I, breathing into the closed-circuit sets, were each carrying fifty pounds; with me on one rope was Annullu, and with Hardie, Urkien; the loads of the Sherpas were fully as heavy as ours, and they were using no oxygen.

At first we gained height steadily. When we had rounded the north end of the great ice-cliff, we were on the snow-slope that we had reached when we found a site for Camp 3 on May 4th. Breathing oxygen from the closed-circuit sets, we did not find the weight on our backs too heavy, and we kicked steps in rather soft snow to the foot of a steeper slope of ice. Here we had to cut steps for a hundred feet to the top of the slope, where there was a snow-filled crevasse which offered a resting-place. We sat there for a little, our axes driven into the snow lodging on the gentler slope above the crevasse. Directly above was another ice-slope, and we avoided this by bearing to the right over deep snow which filled a depression between two ice-bulges. Two hundred feet higher, we were above these, and at the foot of a long ice-slope rising obliquely towards the upper edge of the south flank of the icefall. On our right, the ice-slope ended suddenly where the south flank of the icefall plunged down towards the Yalung; on our left, the north flank of the icefall fell away more gently towards the Valley, broken into a confusion of ice-cliffs. Three hundred feet directly above us the ice-slope ended against an ice-cliff, but its most southerly part, above and slightly to the right of us, seemed to continue round the corner of that cliff. What happened there we could not see. At our feet the ice was granular, easy to cut; higher up, near the top of the slope, it glistened, promising to be glassy.

The Yalung face from the west

Cutting steps all the way, we reached the top of the slope, rounded the corner, and found ourselves in a snow-filled recess with a drop on our right down to the Yalung, a sheer ice-cliff ahead, and a snow-slope leading up to our left to the foot of a sharp forty-foot rise. Hardie drove his axe into the snow to secure my rope, and I began first to kick and then to cut steps up to the shelf above this rise. The snow higher up was hard, and by cutting holds for the hands as well as for the feet I soon reached to within a few feet of the top of the wall. The oxygen enabled me to work hard, though with more distress than if I had been doing the same thing with such a load in the Alps at, say, 12,000 feet. Suddenly, as I was cutting the last few steps, I felt as if a firm hand had been clapped over my mouth and nose: I could not breathe. I found later that the rubber lining of the mask had worked loose and when I breathed in was wrapping itself round my face, but all I knew at the moment was that I was being suffocated. Already breathless, and in an awkward position on a steep face, I felt desperate; hanging on with one hand, I tore the mask off my face with the other. Thank God, I thought, for fresh air, and I panted and panted, unendingly it seemed, because the air here, though I could now have as much as I wanted, was pretty thin. It was only a few steps to the top of the wall, and I had already cut them. I reached up with one hand and stuck the shaft of the axe into the snow above the wall: it went in about six inches and was firm. I dug the gloved fingers of my other hand into the snow beside it and hauled myself over the top. All I wanted was to be where I could lie down and get my breath back. In a few minutes I had recovered enough to tear the rubber lining out of the mask and to connect the set again. I went a few feet farther up the slope, drove in my axe, and brought up Annullu. Hardie and Urkien followed.

We were now on a level ice-platform, twenty feet wide and fifty yards long. Above was a crevasse, then a steep slope, part snow, part ice, and above that again a great wall of ice, in places a hundred feet high. It stretched across the whole width of our front, the last barrier below the Shelf.

To our left it was less high, because a snow-slope ran up into a recess in it. At the apex of the snow-slope the wall was only forty feet high, and formed a right-angled re-entrant corner, overhanging at the bottom. We reached it up some very unstable slopes: they were steep, and seamed with crevasses; the ice was rotten, and the overlying snow untrustworthy. We moved one at a time to a ledge under the overhang at the foot of the final corner. The wall on our right as we looked up the corner was just off the vertical, and made of excellent snow. Hardie, while Urkien belayed him, cut up it, moving left towards the angle of the corner as he climbed higher and the wall grew steeper. Then he was up, and drawing in Urkien's rope. When Annullu and I joined them, we found that we were on a gently sloping snow-field above the highest of the cliffs of the Upper Icefall. We tramped up through soft deep snow over a curve of the slope, and saw the Great Shelf before us, and at our level; but for the moment we could see no way to it. Immediately in front of us were crevasses and seracs, a tangle of angular ice-blocks and pinnacles separated by chasms, the region that marks the bending over of the ice at the edge of the Shelf and the top of the icefall. This zone was a hundred yards across, and we could not to-day, looking at it, tell whether or not there was a way through to the Shelf. We had been going over five hours; the Sherpas, who had been breathing nothing but the thin air, were very tired; we decided to camp where we were.

In some ways it was a good site; it was nearly level, and it was perfectly safe from avalanche; but it was exposed; there was always wind at Camp 4. We guessed its height at 23,500 feet.

We pitched our one tent and saw off the Sherpas on their

way down to Camp 3. It was blowing hard, and sheets of snow-dust swept continually past the tent. We spent the rest of the day, as was usual at high camps, in our bags melting snow to make drinks, and later slowly producing an evening meal.

Now, half-way through our test of the closed-circuit oxygen sets, we discussed the day's findings. We were in agreement. We had appreciated the energy given us by the high concentration of oxygen, but we both felt that we had done a very hard day's work, and we had felt, too, that where climbing was difficult the voluminous apparatus was an encumbrance, that it hampered us when we were, for example, balancing in, and cutting, steps on steep ice. Moreover, in a way less easily defined, we had felt the apparatus cut us off from the world around us, and from each other. These were the impressions after only one day's use; but further experience did not lead us to change them. We had not actively enjoyed climbing, in marked contrast to later occasions, when we repeated the climb with the open-circuit sets, going more slowly, but thoroughly enjoying ourselves, and in contrast also to the experience of Streather and Mather, and of MacKinnon and Jackson, who at various times made this same journey without either type of set, and reported that they had had some of the most enjoyable climbing of their lives.

It was a wild night, but by eight-fifteen we were both asleep. At first we were breathing oxygen: we had a cylinder between us, and the gas ran through a T-piece to our two masks. It made us warm and comfortable; but it was finished by 1 a.m., and I woke at once. A half-wakeful period followed: I lay warm and drowsy, going over plans and feeling sanguine; everything seemed to be going well: I was still feeling the effects of my few hours of sleep with oxygen. Then I slept once more, and woke feeling wretched; I was listless, depressed, cold, hating the thought of moving to light the stove or do anything which brought nearer the time to start out:

the effect of the oxygen had worn off. Hardie noticed exactly the same thing.

There was snow everywhere inside the tent: during the night we had left one of the sleeve-entrances slightly open, and powder snow had blown in and now covered everything. Between six-thirty and seven-thirty Hardie put together our oxygen sets, which we had kept in the tent with us all night. Outside all was grey; it was still blowing hard; it looked as if it was going to snow.

When the two sets were ready, Hardie turned on his oxygen. There was a loud hissing sound as the oxygen leaked out. The valve was frozen, and refused to seal when turned on. Several times he tried to screw it firmly into the open position but still the gas hissed out. The tap was cold and stiff; fingers and hands lost their feeling; it was hard work even trying to turn the tap. After half an hour he turned off the taps and said we must warm up the cylinders before we could use them. He warmed his hands over the stove and put them over the valve. I took my whole cylinder into my sleeping-bag and stuck it between my legs; made as it was of steel, it felt a good deal colder than a lump of ice. At last, by eight-thirty, the valves were thawed enough for us to open the taps without leakage, and at eight-fifty we made a start. The day was improving, a surprise, because days as a rule started well and grew worse, and a day that started badly usually stayed bad. But today the wind died down and the sun began to shine.

As we looked towards the Shelf, the seracs before us seemed least broken on the left, so we started by going northwards, towards Kangchenjunga West. Here we could see a long serac lying on its side. It looked like a whale about a hundred yards long and a hundred feet high, lying with its tail on our small snow-field and its head towards the Shelf. It offered a way through at least the first crevasses. We cut steps up onto the whaleback and walked along its crest to its far end. Here there was an abrupt drop of twenty feet, a few crevasses, and what looked like a corridor of snow leading between ice-blocks to the Shelf. I belayed on the whaleback while Hardie cut down to the valley of blocks and crevasses below. We ploughed through the snow-corridor beyond, and were on the Great Shelf.

It was huge, and seemed almost flat. Before us it rose gently to the foot of the cliffs that fall from the south ridge of the mountain. To our left it rose gently northwards, at about fifteen degrees, towards the foot of the Gangway. Though evidently very steep just below the foot of the Gangway, it seemed, as far as we could see, to have no obstacles at all: no large crevasses, no ice-cliffs. We thought that it looked, after the slopes we had been on, like an enormous football-field, but on a bit of a slant. It was now ten o'clock, and we determined to go as far up it as we could to find a place for Camp 5.

We took it in turns to plod first through the snow. It was knee-deep, but progress was steady. Some way below the foot of the Gangway the slope began to steepen. To our left, to the west, was the edge of the Shelf, the ice-cliffs overlooking the steep Valley. Ahead were the slopes under the west col of Kangchenjunga. High on these we saw the red rocks of the Sickle, the east end of which bent down as a bare wall separating the snow-filled hollow under the Sickle from the Gangway farther east. At the lower end of that wall the snow of the Gangway and that of the hollow under the Sickle merged into one wide slope of snow and ice, broken in places by ice-cliffs which came down to form the north end of the Great Shelf. We were now at the foot of these slopes, where they steepened to forty degrees, and the snow was harder.

In air-photographs we had seen on these slopes a broad ledge under an ice-cliff, about four hundred feet below the foot of the Gangway; now we were able to pick out this ledge and cliff easily, and, thinking it a likely place for our Camp 5, we headed for it. The slopes directly below it were precipitous, a region of seracs, and those to the east, though unbroken, seemed likely to receive any fall of rock or snow from the south face of the mountain above; so we chose to approach by a line farther west, aiming in the direction of the snow-basin under the Sickle. The slope steepened still more, until, three hundred feet below the ledge for which we were heading, we were on a slope of ice at fifty degrees. Its angle varied slightly from place to place, and sometimes it was bare, sometimes covered by two to six inches of floury snow. The ledge was three hundred feet higher, and a rather greater distance horizontally to our right. We traversed across the slope, both of us having trouble with our oxygen masks. They did not seem to fit properly now, and oxygen leaked out under our chins; they were in the way of the climbing. The slope seemed very steep, and there was a small ice-cliff below as we traversed: it would be a long way to climb back if we fell off here. By the time we reached the shelf we looked on the oxygen sets as nothing but a nuisance, forgetting that but for them we should never have come here so fast. It was only eleven forty-five.

The ledge was all we wanted. It was high enough, about 25,300 feet; it was almost level; there was room for a dozen tents had we wanted them; and it was sheltered by the ice-cliff above it, which was a hundred feet high and stable, from danger of snow-avalanches off the slopes below the Sickle, a protection for which later we were to be thankful. We sat on it side by side, our backs free of the weight of the oxygen apparatus, our masks off 'for a breath of fresh air', our goggles pushed up to look at the view. All the valleys were in cloud. Over the Talung Saddle we could look across the sea of cloud covering Darjeeling. Due south was Kabru, a thousand feet below us; south-west, cloud over the Yalung, and beyond it, cloud over India; due west, Jannu, a great fang, its top now level with us, and to the north of it, and far away, Makalu. For a moment, on our ledge, we felt like aviators in the nose of their ship, above the world.

There was no time to lose. We now had, at most, two weeks in which to make practicable for porters the route we had found to the Shelf, to stock Camps 4 and 5, to find a place near 27,000 feet for Camp 6, and to reach the final ridge. We stayed for fifteen minutes, then hurried down. In forty minutes we were back at Camp 4, where we discarded our oxygen sets, and in an hour from Camp 4 we were down at Camp 3; to climb this same distance had taken us nearly eight hours, five on the first day, nearly three on the second.

At Camp 3 we found Streather and Mather; they had come up to stay, and we told them the story, and what had to be done on the route to Camp 4. It was far from ready for a big caravan of Sherpas: in at least four places it would need fixed ropes, and there were many steps to be cut on the ice-slopes.

We spoke to Brown at Camp 1 and told him our news; then we heard him relay the news to those at Base, with whom from here we were not able on this night to speak directly. Next day I was down at Base myself.

Now, before our final climbs, I wanted everyone who could be spared to have at least two nights at Base before starting up. Streather and Mather had to stay at Camp 3 with five Sherpas, to work on the route to Camp 4. The rest of us gathered at Base on May 14th, the day on which the last carry over the Hump had been completed, and I explained the plans for the next two weeks.

There were four tasks: the stocking of Camp 4, and the preparation of the route there; the stocking of Camp 5, the base for the work on the last three thousand feet of the mountain; the placing of Camp 6 as high as possible, if possible not more than a thousand feet from the top; and the exploration of the final ridge.

Streather and Mather, who were sleeping at Camp 3, were now improving the route to Camp 4. There were ropes to be fixed on the steep walls immediately below Camp 4; and on the ice-slope below those walls we planned to have a long rope anchored with ice-pitons at intervals of about thirty feet. Here, too, the steps already made would have to be renewed and made larger. It would take two, perhaps three, days before this work was done and a carry of loads went through to Camp 4. Six loads of food, kerosene and oxygen, had to go to Camp 4 from 3; and in the event, Streather and Mather reached Camp 4 on May 15th. On the two days that followed, since there was not time for them to come down to Base to rest, they rested, with good effect, at Camp 3, 21,800 feet.

The second task, the stocking of Camp 5, was in some ways our hardest. The Sherpas would have to carry there without oxygen; we could not use for it six of the best of them, whom I wanted to hold for the carrying later of the highest camp of all; eleven loads, each of more than thirty pounds, had to be taken up; and it was a vital step. MacKinnon and Jackson were to be responsible for it, with Annullu, an exceptionally strong and capable man, to lead their party of eleven Sherpas. They were to start from Base next day, May 15th, and go easily to Camp 3, where their loads were waiting for them, sleeping on the way one night at Camp 1 and another at Camp 2.

From Camp 3 they would carry in one day to Camp 4, and the next day to Camp 5, the four hundred-odd pounds destined for Camp 5. They would leave these loads at Camp 5, and come down that same day to Camp 3, passing on the way Band and Brown, who were to be the first to try to reach the final ridge, and those of us who were to help them to carry their top camp, Mather and I and four Sherpas, Dawa Tenzing, Ang Temba, Tashi and Ang Norbu.

The eight of us were to leave Base one day after the party carrying to Camp 5, and to follow them all the way, one day behind, reaching Camp 5 on the day after it had been stocked. From there we should have to find the way and at the same time carry to Camp 6 near the top of the Gangway, where we would leave Band and Brown, ourselves returning to Camp 5. Following us from Camp 3 at a day's interval would be the second summit-ridge pair, Hardie and Streather, and with them, to carry their additional food and oxygen to Camp 6, two of our best Sherpas, Urkien and Ila Tenzing. They would go up to Camp 6 on the day after Band and Brown, while all at Camp 5 would go down except Dawa Tenzing and me. We two would wait there, first for Urkien and Ila Tenzing, then for Band and Brown, last for Hardie and Streather.

While the first pair was high, MacKinnon and Jackson, with those Sherpas still able to go with them, would make a second, replenishing, lift to Camp 5, to give us more reserve of food and fuel there in case of accident or delay, and to be themselves at hand if needed.

I planned that every European going above Camp 3 should, until his main job was done, climb with an open-circuit oxygen set, and use oxygen for sleeping, and that every Sherpa carrying above Camp 5 should do so using an open-circuit set. This meant the carriage to Camp 5 of more than two hundred pounds weight of oxygen cylinders alone, so that the difficulty of stocking Camp 5 was greatly increased; but it was thoroughly worth while when it came to placing Camp 6, and resulted in twelve men reaching that camp, at nearly 27,000 feet, with comparatively little trouble.

This programme was open to some variation. The weather was unreliable, and we expected hitches. To adjust our plan to these, we allowed throughout a small extra margin of food, of fuel and of oxygen; and for the making known of changes, we relied on the 'walkie-talkie' radios. Of these, there would be one each at Camps 5, 4, 3, and Base. At Base would be our radio-receiver, by which we obtained our weather forecasts, and here, at the time of the final climbs, John Clegg would wait, to send to us the weather reports from India and to keep us in touch with Darjeeling.

23 Camp 3   Looking down to the Hump, the Hump gully, and the Plateau

If all went well and there were no delays, the second pair should make its highest climb on May 23rd. Two days later, we should all be off the mountain. If, as was probable, there were delays of a day here and a day there, we should still be down well before the month was out.

24 The Upper Icefall   Below Camp 3

CHAPTER TEN

CAMP FIVE

May 15th–May 22nd

WE now had three days of fair weather.
MacKinnon, Jackson and their party started on the afternoon of May 15th; Annullu was already at Camp 3. The eleven Sherpas were pleased and excited, knowing that they had been picked for important work, and were going where none of them had been. Their packs were all but empty, since most of the stores for Camp 5 were already at Camp 3; and their light loads and eager step gave them a strong, buoyant look.

We were to follow at a day's interval: Joe Brown and George Band, the first summit-ridge pair; John Clegg, Norman Hardie and I; and four of the Sherpas chosen to go to the highest camp, Dawa Tenzing himself, Ang Temba, Ang Norbu, and old Tashi, kind, serious, gentle, and faithful, on the high snows a tiger.

We reached Camp 1 on May 16th, at about four-thirty. Below us the valley was full of thick white cloud, against which our red and yellow flags were vivid. We were in sunshine. The afternoon was warm, clear and serene; the hard snow sparkled; opposite us was the east face of Jannu, seven thousand feet of precipice coated with blue-green, fluted ice.

Next morning also was clear. We started at seven-thirty, and found the track hard and sound, easy to travel. We stopped often to take photographs. The rays of the early sun glistened on the sweep of snow, showing its texture by shadow and light; our windproofs were spots of gay colour, George Band's bright yellow, Joe Brown's bright blue, and Norman Hardie's bright red.

There was a change already in the upper part of the Lower Icefall. The bergschrund at its edge had first been crossed by means of a stout bridge of snow and ice, debris which at this point was lodged in its mouth. Later, as the bridge began to melt, we had reinforced it with a ladder. Now only the ladder was left, and we had to belay each man across it carefully.

From the top of the Hump we had had a long look at the Upper Icefall. We were falling in love with our route: the smooth steepness west of the Hump; the intricate corner at the top of the Lower Icefall; the complexity of the Upper Icefall, its blues and whites and long shapely lines; beyond, the broad recess of the Shelf, under the red rocks of the summit ridges. Beautiful from far away, the mountain was beautiful also from here.

On the morning of the 18th the party above us were to have started at eight. From Camp 2 we watched their camp through glasses, and saw no sign of life except an occasional hooded figure slipping from tent to tent. After a good deal of shouting we brought them to the radio, and heard that one of their Sherpas, pleading a headache, would go no higher. Finally they started without him, at nine; Streather, Urkien, and Ila Tenzing going with them for the day. We caught only glimpses of them. It was cloudy now and windy. The old wind of late April seemed to have come back. Clouds raced eastwards over the ridges. Down in the valley, too, it seemed to be windy: the small clouds there moved ceaselessly, billowing suddenly up to our level, twisting, expanding, vanishing.

We moved up to Camp 3, where we slept, some in a cave, some in large green Meade tents of the kind that the wind had ripped at Corner Camp. The first half of the night was wakeful for us all, partly because of altitude, partly no doubt because

of excitement; the second half was very wild; I wondered sometimes if our tents would stand it.

Remembering the difficulties here of the other party, I
called the Sherpas at four-thirty. About five-thirty Joe Brown
went outside, and reported three separate layers of grey, filmy
cloud. We all felt ill, and gloomy. The wind howled round the
tents, driving the snow in furious gusts. Norman Hardie and
Neil Mather assembled the oxygen sets, a grim struggle with
the cold. It was, after all, nine when we started. We left Hardie
and Streather here.

Breathing open-circuit oxygen, we felt better. The track
was now good: the snow was firm, and ropes were fixed on the
steep walls. We came up in four hours, reaching Camp 4 at
two-thirty. For once, the afternoon was clear, and we could
see all round, from Kabru in the south to Everest in the north-
west; Jannu, almost due west, seemed close by.

Of the party above us we could at first see nothing. Then, at
a quarter to three, we saw some of them about three hundred
feet below Camp 5, and still climbing. We were dismayed: they
should have been there long ago. We did not know what a late
start they had had, nor how much plugging through soft snow.
Three-quarters of an hour later some of them were there still,
with Tom MacKinnon.

At four-thirty the first of the Sherpas came slowly into
camp: they were Annullu, Phurchita and Hlakpa Sonar, our
young Ang Temba's father. They were followed soon by a rope
of four: Da Tsering, Gyalgen, Jackson and Changjup. These
Sherpas were among our toughest, but to-night they were very
tired. Jackson, dog-tired, was three-quarters blind; he was
unable to tell much of what had been done; but it seemed that
most of the stores had been carried to some place near Camp 5,
if not right to it. We heard his story only later: at the moment
we were too much concerned about the men still on the Shelf.
There was nothing to be seen of them, so Annullu went down

with the other Sherpas who had returned, leaving Jackson with us. He told us that his sight was much better: he could now see the feet of a man walking in front of him, and he had on the way down noticed a bridge over a crevasse which that morning he had crossed unaware of its existence. We made room for him in a tent, between Band and me.

At five-fifteen three more Sherpas arrived: Pasang Sonar, Ang Dawa from Kunde, and Mingma Tenzing, Dawa Tenzing's son. With words of praise and encouragement, we hurried them on down: they had not much time if they were to reach Camp 3 before dark.

There was still no sign of Tom MacKinnon and Pemi Dorje, and Joe Brown, Neil Mather and I set out for the whaleback serac to look for them. We had gone only a few paces when they appeared on top of the serac, and started down its sloping crest towards us. Coming downhill, they moved faster than we, and in the five minutes that it took us to walk, panting, uphill fifty yards, they reached us. Pemi Dorje was in front. He was tied to Tom MacKinnon with a double length of thin avalanche-cord; by means of it, on the far side of the whaleback, Tom had just hauled him out of a crevasse into which he had fallen over his head, only stopping himself by spreading his legs. He swayed in his tracks, and before he reached the tents sank to his knees. Tom was tired too, though nothing like beaten. He was a wild-looking figure. He was excited, and, for him, voluble. Almost at once he was telling us that he meant to come up with us to-morrow to see that the carry was properly completed.

We had four two-man tents, and we were now eleven; for plainly there was no question of these two going on. Tom MacKinnon went to the tent that Mather was sharing with Brown; Pemi Dorje into one of the tents of the Sherpas. Night was falling.

Next day we heard their story. MacKinnon and Jackson, above Camp 3, had been wearing open-circuit oxygen sets.

97

The Upper Icefall, near to Camp 4

By now, few of the masks of these sets fitted well: we had lost too much weight, and our cheeks were sunken. As Jackson climbed from Camp 3 to Camp 4 on May 18th, his breath had leaked out round the bridge of his nose and fogged his dark glasses. Many times in the day, unable to keep them wiped clear, he had pushed them onto his forehead in sunlight so bright that its glare on the snow forced even a man wearing glasses to screw up his eyes a little. Before he reached camp his eyes were beginning to prick, and in the tent he found himself 'snow-blind'. All night he lay awake, turning this way and that, now sitting up, now lying down, seeking relief; his eyes seemed to be on fire. In the morning he could hardly bear to open the lids, and he could see only the blurred outline of his hand when he moved it before his face. MacKinnon did his best to persuade him to stay in camp: not only could he not see, but there was a risk of further damage to his eyes. Jackson would not be persuaded: blind though he was, he could still carry a load, and if tied in the middle of a rope could still give encouragement. He had his way.

At about nine o'clock, ready to start, MacKinnon found that the Sherpas, thinking their loads too heavy to carry to Camp 5, had discarded several important pieces of equipment, which now lay on the snow. Loads had to be repacked, and the start was not made till ten-twenty. MacKinnon and Jackson each carried thirty pounds in addition to their oxygen sets. MacKinnon led the first rope, Phurchita led the second, with Jackson in the middle of the rope, and Changjup led the third. They were already very late.

The first two ropes passed over the whaleback serac and through to the Shelf without mishap, but Changjup, while letting a man down from the top of the serac, lost his load. It had been slung from his forehead by a headband only, and had slipped out of the band and rolled down the south side of the whaleback. This slope was of snow-ice, and convex; once the load had started, it was for the time being lost. It shot down, partly disintegrating on the way, and came into sight rolling down the slope above Camp 4, where at last it came to rest. There was no point in going on without a load; the others on his rope must not be delayed; the load must be taken up. Before MacKinnon and Annullu could return to stop him, Changjup untied himself, and climbed down the whaleback and down the slope below. It was a long way down and a long pull back: by the time he had gathered up the scattered contents of his pack, made all fast, and returned to the top of the whaleback, the three ropes were far ahead. Alone, he climbed down from the end of the whaleback to the spur of ice by which we bridged the crevasse beyond, crossed that, and several more crevasses, and reached the Shelf. Here, a solitary figure, far behind, he followed in the wake of the party until, two-thirds of the way to Camp 5, he met the first of the returning ropes. He went on a little, and then met the second returning rope. Jackson, who was on this rope, induced him to leave his load here and to come down. It was after four o'clock.

On the Shelf every rope had found the going hard. Each man was carrying about forty pounds, and the snow was soft and deep, sometimes knee-deep. MacKinnon's rope had gradually pulled ahead, and had been the first to reach the foot of the steep slopes below Camp 5. The ropes behind had been slower, in spite of having the trail made for them. As MacKinnon described it, "We were at it the whole time. There were no long halts. It was twelve steps and a rest, and twelve steps and another rest." Now and then someone would slip out of his rope because he could not keep up, and would overtake the others later when they had halted longer.

All the steps up the ice to Camp 5 were cut by MacKinnon. His oxygen, and Jackson's, had finished half-way over the Great Shelf. He, Hlakpa Sonar, and Phurchita reached the site of the camp at a quarter to three. A quarter of an hour later Annullu and Da Tsering joined them. Jackson, who for some of the time had been on their rope, had unroped at the foot of the steepest section, and waited there, sitting in the snow, eyes closed: it would not have been safe for him to balance, half-blind, up the long line of ice-steps. Already, on a steep slope, the Sherpas had had to place his feet for him.

After pitching the tent on the ledge at Camp 5, anchoring the guys to oxygen bottles laid on the snow, and putting our other stores in the tent, the first four Sherpas started down, picking up Jackson at the foot of the ice-slope, and Changjup some way down the Great Shelf. MacKinnon stayed where he was, waiting for the last of the Sherpas, Ang Dawa, Mingma Tenzing, Pasang Sonar and Pemi Dorje. At four o'clock they were still sixty yards from camp, separated from it by the ice of the rising traverse, difficult and exposed. So tired were they now, and so slow, that MacKinnon decided they must cache their loads where they were if they were to reach Camp 3 before dark. He climbed down to them, and they dug holes for their loads on the slope. Then, all five on one rope, they started down.

The day before, Pemi Dorje had been more tired than anyone else; MacKinnon had given him oxygen, and had helped him with his load. This day, on the climb up, he had gone well, but when they started down he could not go as fast as the others on the rope, and MacKinnon had stayed behind with him. Tired though he was, he was still cheerful: he was smiling and apologizing for being slow and clumsy.

Inside our tent it was crowded. Band and I, who were to sleep with oxygen, each had his oxygen set in the tent; Jackson lay between us, his head at our feet; beside me was our radio set. At seven o'clock I was given the weather forecast by Clegg, at Base: "Wind west to south-west; forty knots. Temperature in free air at 20–25,000 feet one to five degrees Fahrenheit." Normally our winds were north-westerly, and the temperatures

25 Jannu from Camp 3

26 The Yalung face from the west

See page

Photo. Indian Air F

The west ridge from the air

See page 123
Photo. Indian Air Force

28 The rocks on the south-west face   Band on May 25th. '*traversed to the right again acr*
a slabby face'.

below zero; the change was ominous. It blew hard all night, and we woke to a wild dawn. The wind was fierce, and there was a blizzard. Outside the tents we could see only a few yards. We found Jackson curled up in a ball at the bottom of the tent, between our feet. He had been in pain all night, relieved only partly by doses of aspirin, but now he was more comfortable than he had been for two days.

At ten o'clock it seemed that Jackson, MacKinnon and Pemi Dorje should at least make a start down, and slowly they began to get ready. Half an hour later I went out to look round: it was still blowing and snowing hard, the new snow was a foot deep by the tents in spite of the gale, and as soon as I stepped off the beaten platform I sank in at once up to my knees. I decided that they had better wait. Later, I went out again, with Tashi, to look at the track; we put on the rope and went a little way down towards the highest fixed rope. The new snow, about a foot deep, rested on a layer of old soft snow, and slid off when disturbed. In a few yards we lost sight of the camp and of the flag near it which marked the route; during the stronger gusts we could see nothing at all, and crouched in the snow until they died down. We went back to camp and Tashi spent some time trying to dig out our tents: the snow had piled up so much on the windward side of them that we could hardly see them, and the occupants were pushed gradually towards the lee side, the roof and walls sagging in under the weight of snow. From inside it was impossible to push it away: it merely packed hard under your hand, and was then there for good. Tashi had a plate and scooped it away as best he could from outside, but the gale blew it back again, and half his effort was wasted.

Inside the tents we brewed tea or lemonade, ate occasional biscuits, now and then opened a tin of sardines. It is difficult at these heights to get enough to drink; to supply drink enough for the whole party we had to keep our stoves going all day.

That night we did not use oxygen, and lay awake, sleepless

much of the time, but comfortable. Rime formed on the inside of the tent from the condensation of our breath, and was shaken off in showers onto our sleeping-bags by the wind flapping the tent canvas. In the morning the wind was north-westerly and violent; the peaks were hidden by layers of grey cloud, below which, during a lull, far to the south and west, we caught a glimpse of cumulus cloud in sunlight. I wrote, "In the tents, which are half-buried in drifting snow, it is a shambles. Oxygen cylinders—sopping wet sleeping-bags—snow everywhere—bundles of wet Duvet clothes—at night the torch swinging wildly hung from the tent roof."

At ten-thirty next morning Jackson, MacKinnon and Pemi Dorje started down, escorted by Band and Brown as far as the bottom of the upper ice-cliffs below Camp 4. There had been a slight break in the blizzard, but it looked as if there was much more snow to come, and soon it was thick again. I retired to my sleeping-bag, where I found that it took an hour to warm up after the few minutes I had spent outside in seeing the party off. Outside, from time to time, it was now possible to see Kabru and Jannu, grey and surrounded by mists; at hand the snow drove past; the wind battered and tore at the tent.

That night we used oxygen again, and slept. Tashi lit the stove at five-thirty a.m. and, going out to visit the other pair of tents, suddenly announced that it was a clear morning: he could see all round, he said, from Darjeeling to Everest; the only clouds were small and far down in the valleys.

It is an hour before the first cup of tea is ready. What do you do in that time? Very little; spend perhaps some of it in talking yourself to the point of making a move; perhaps you write a few lines of diary, or, very determined, begin while still in your sleeping-bag to prepare your oxygen set. This morning, some porridge was made, which no one could finish; we washed down a few biscuits with a second pint of tea.

Outside, instead of the neat tents and stacked loads of two days before, we saw a streamlined snowscape, the tents half submerged, the snow heaped in drifts in the lee of them. Here an ice-axe stuck out, only a few inches of it showing, someone's crampons tied to its head; there we saw the corner of a ration-box, or of a kerosene tin; of oxygen bottles and ropes there was no sign.

The first thing was to find our gear. We started scraping away the snow, only to find that much of it was packed hard. There was no way of telling where anything was, and digging at random was tiring us before the day's work began. A blow of the axe drove the blade in only about a foot, so that all that was explored was a strip of snow two inches wide and a foot deep; and every blow had to be followed by a pause, for the recovery of breath and resolution. One by one missing crampons and oxygen bottles were dug up, until at last we had them all. The tent that we were to carry to Camp 5 was struck and packed. We were almost ready. Someone started to uncoil a rope, and I looked round. Where are the other ropes? More digging. Slowly we realized that there might not be any more ropes. We ought to have kept them in the tents; we ought to have counted them when MacKinnon's men went down. It was easy to say it now, but none of us before had known a blizzard which could so change the face of a camp as this had done, and forethought is not a conspicuous quality at 23,000 feet. Nor is quickness to learn: strange as it seems now, we were to make much the same mistake two days later.

We had one rope. Search as we might we could not find another, and rather than waste time in further search, I sent Dawa Tenzing and Tashi down to bring up a spare coil of manila rope which we had left at the top of the fixed rope just below camp. While they fetched it, Joe Brown and I started, with Ang Temba and Ang Norbu, to break the trail. It was ten-fifteen.

Ang Temba and Ang Norbu were tied in the middle of the rope, and Joe Brown and I took it in turns to go first. We climbed onto the whaleback, crossed the seracs and crevasses beyond it, and reached the Great Shelf at eleven-thirty. We ploughed slowly up it; the snow was to our knees; Joe Brown and I were breathing oxygen and each carrying his personal gear, Lilo, sleeping-bag, and spare clothes. Ang Temba had a bundle of flags on sticks; every seventy-five yards I hauled a flag from the bundle and stuck it into the snow beside the trail, and at every second flag we sat down for five minutes and changed the lead. After all the new snow, there was no sign of old tracks on the surface, though sometimes we could find the hard-trodden layer underneath; we tried to keep to it, guessing its general direction and feeling for it with our feet.

Though the blizzard had stopped, the wind was almost as strong as ever; all day it blew from the north-west, from our left front; often we had to stop altogether, crouching in the snow before it, our faces buried in our hands to ward off the sting of the driven snow.

We were going more slowly than MacKinnon's party, and the Sherpas, who were using no oxygen here, were having a harder time of it than we. As the day wore on, halts, and requests for halts, became more frequent; but they persevered, and our halts were as often to rest ourselves from trail-breaking as to rest them. Approaching the upper part of the Shelf, we saw a box sticking out of the snow: it was Changjup's load, a box of Sherpa rations. We took out the essentials, sugar and milk, and Joe Brown crammed them into his sack. A little farther there was another box, empty, and a Primus stove; we picked up the stove. The slope now was steepening rapidly: we were at the foot of the rise of four or five hundred feet to Camp 5, snow at the bottom, ice at the top. In the snow before us we saw a yellow oxygen bottle and part of a tent; all around us the snow was rough, in lumps of all shapes and sizes, here packed and there

Camp 6

soft and unstable, the unmistakable debris of a recent avalanche. It began to be clear that the avalanche, of new snow piled by the blizzard on the slope under the Sickle, must have carried away MacKinnon's cache from the bare slope near Camp 5. We were too tired fully to realize now the magnitude of the possible disaster, and we plodded wearily towards the wreckage, while I tried to remember what had been cached and what had been taken right through to camp. I could not remember clearly, and wondered what we would do if we had no tents, no kerosene, no oxygen. I picked up the oxygen bottle, which was one of our large ones, and stuck it on top of my pack. A few feet higher was a tent; we were on a forty-degree slope of snow into which we sank easily, and which slipped down under us; at last we reached the tent, and Joe Brown added it to his load; a little farther was another tent, which went onto mine. Scattered about us were small pieces of gear, including a dish-cloth.

To collect these we had turned a little to the right, off our course, and now we headed up and to the left. The slope was forty-five degrees, the snow not firm, and some of it slabby, on top of harder snow-ice; at intervals there were narrow crevasses; sometimes there was a stretch of hard glistening snow-ice, blown bare of surface snow, up which we could go in crampons without floundering, but by now we were all carrying stray bits of equipment, and our progress was funereal. My oxygen finished, and suddenly I felt the utter exhaustion which invariably follows the cutting off of the supply: my load seemed a mountain. Joe Brown's oxygen gave out a few minutes later, and we scraped a seat in the slope; the Sherpas did the same, easing their loads off their backs. The other four were below us, near the place where we had picked up the tents.

We still had two hundred feet of climbing across a slope steep and exposed; the wind raced across it, driving the snow. All steps had vanished. I decided to use some of the precious oxygen in the bottle we had picked up: I could use it to cut across to camp, and then share the same bottle that night with Joe Brown instead of using another full bottle. We dumped one of the salvaged tents here for Band to bring on; I took the other, turned on the gas and started cutting.

As we went on, the slope steepened. There was now no sign of MacKinnon's cache, but half-way we saw something black in the snow fifty feet down; we thought at first that it was a stone dropped from the crags of the Sickle, then, looking more carefully, recognized one of our radios. It was precious, almost indispensable for our changing plans, but it was fifty feet down. It looked to-day as if it was going to take everything we had to reach camp. We let it lie.

I could rest my left hand comfortably on the slope. I would cut two steps, one for my right foot, one for my left, dig the pick of my axe in the slope, holding it across my body to steady the balance, and haul myself up the two steps I had cut; then rest. After a few breaths I was ready to cut two more. So it went on. Now and then I heard the rush of the wind approaching, and I would stop cutting for a moment and use both hands and the axe to help me to stay in my steps. I did not look behind: I had a mental picture of the three men near exhaustion, all without oxygen, all heavily burdened. At any moment one of them through fatigue might make a false step; there was nothing to be done about it; it was too hard a slope to drive in the shaft of the axe for a belay; we had to get over as best we could, wasting no time, and hanging on when the strong gusts came. At four-fifteen we reached Camp 5.

From the top of the ice-slope we had a descent of twenty feet to the camp-site. We walked down, the high ice-cliff on our left, and saw before us what at first glance seemed a bare shelf: it looked exactly as when Hardie and I had been here nine days earlier. Where was our camp? Then we saw the very tip of a tent sticking out of the snow. The avalanche which had swept clear the ice we had just crossed and carried away our dump there had swept also round the side of our protecting ice-cliff and buried our tent and stores left on the west end of the ledge. Farther along, protected by the main cliff, the ledge was clear: if we camped five yards farther along we should be perfectly safe. In the meantime there was more digging to be done. We had not yet enough shelter, nor any fuel, and night was coming.

If the digging had been hard in the morning, it was harder now. The snow was packed so tight that the tent might have been frozen in, and we had to be careful not to tear the cloth. We ourselves were so tired as hardly to be able to stand: we staggered about like drunken men, tormented by the fierce gusts of wind that every few moments tore across the ledge, lifting and whirling the new snow. At last the tent was dug up; we found a ration-box at the end of one of the guy-ropes, and two oxygen cylinders at the end of the other; inside it was a second tent, in its bag, not unpacked. Then Joe found a two-gallon tin of kerosene.

By now the second rope had arrived. I watched them come down the last few feet to the ledge: their faces were grey-blue, their cheeks sunken; icicles hung from their nostrils and froth bubbled at their lips as they breathed; they could hardly stand, and swayed as they walked. While Joe continued his search in the snow, and found ten of our small blue oxygen cylinders, the rest of us set about pitching the tents, which were part filled with snow, wrestling with them in a wind that sometimes lifted them clear in the air. At one moment, after we had pitched two, tied together end to end and pegged out in the snow, and were just about to put in our gear, a sudden gust lifted both off the ground, whipping out every peg, and left me holding on to one end while the tents flapped in the air like a wind-sock. It was some time since the sun had set

107

behind Kangchenjunga West, and darkness, with its bitter and immediate cold, could not be far off.

At last the tents were up. We swept out the snow, and the Sherpas lit the stoves to melt ice for tea. Brown and I shared a tent pitched end to end with one shared by Dawa Tenzing and Tashi; alongside, the other two tents were joined in the same way. We unpacked outside and pushed the gear in; the sleeping-bags were frozen stiff enough to stand up by themselves. As darkness fell, clouds of steam from the cookers filled the tents, and in our bags our shivering gradually eased.

CHAPTER ELEVEN

CAMP SIX

May 24th

THE wind was strong all night, and when we looked out next morning all was grey, the sky overcast; a bank of hard-packed snow covered the oxygen bottles and ration-boxes that we had left outside to anchor the tents; only the heads of our axes showed above it; the tents themselves were half-buried.

We were now less than three thousand feet below the summit, which lay to the north-east of us. Above camp, to the north, was the Sickle, which, though it was still over fifteen hundred feet above us, seemed close. We could not see the Gangway, which was hidden by the wall of rocks running down from the east end of the Sickle, its 'handle'; but we knew that it was there, a steep corridor leading for nearly two thousand feet to a point on the west ridge of the mountain about three hundred yards from the summit, and less than five hundred feet below it. The foot of the Gangway was not far above us; we could see the broken rocks there, but it was hard to judge the distance, perhaps three hundred feet. Over the foot of the Gangway, to the north-east, we saw precipitous ridges of brown-red rock, the south-west face of the mountain, seamed with ice-filled couloirs, none of which looked easy to climb, and all of which looked as if they might be shoots for falling stones. In that direction, above the rocks and out of sight, was the summit.

We had examined the west ridge and the south-west face carefully from every halt we had ever made in the Yalung, and especially from Base, and had soon realized that while the lower part of the west ridge was jagged and formidable, there was on

Turning off the Gangway, above Camp 6

the south-west face a line of broken rock which started at the Gangway some way below its top, and slanted up towards a snowy spur which joined the main west ridge three or four hundred feet to the west of the summit. It looked as if the route now would be up the Gangway and across those broken rocks, to join the west ridge high up. The rocks would be, as a climber once said, as we found them: there was no guessing if they could be climbed until we were on them. The Gangway was a different problem. Here was a long slope of snow or ice facing south; in all the photographs at our disposal it looked exceedingly steep, and it sloped in two directions, to the south along its own length, and to the west towards the bay below the Sickle. If there was good snow on it, it might offer a highway to the last five hundred feet of the mountain; if it was of ice, it might stop us; if it was of avalanche-snow, it might be a death-trap. Our plan was to gain a footing on it by working through the narrow snow-gullies between the slabby rock outcrops at its foot, and then to carry Camp 6 as high up it as possible. I wanted this camp to be at about 27,000 feet. To carry such a camp would need a strong party and an early start. On the morning of the 23rd we were not a strong party, and an early start was out of the question. We were all tired as a result of the exertions of the day before. We made our first moves in the morning at five, but were nowhere near ready to start by ten. I decided that we must take the risk of delay, and postponed the carrying of Camp 6 for one day. We would spend it here, resting, drinking as much as we could, and making ready every load for the morrow.

We were late up, but we had plenty to do. Dawa Tenzing and Tashi went down to salvage what they could from the avalanche debris below camp; the rest of us dug out once more from the snow about our tents the oxygen bottles which had been dug out the day before and reburied during the night, and made another examination of the rest of the camp-site, probing the snow in case we had missed anything. When all the salvage was counted, and the Sherpas had returned with our radio and two small oxygen bottles, calculation showed that we had just enough to enable us to go on with our first plans. Even the radio was in working order.

We counted the bottles: we had twelve small and three large. We cleaned the snow off the oxygen sets, and put them in the tents ready for the morning start. George Band and Joe Brown chose the food they wanted at the top camp. Luckily it was a still, sunny afternoon. We draped sleeping-bags out on the tents to dry. The temperature rose quickly as soon as the wind dropped, and we sat on boxes, looking at the view. It was the first leisurely enjoyment since leaving Camp 3. Going a few paces below camp, we could scrape a seat in the ice and watch Camp 4. There was no sign of Hardie and Streather, who were to have come up to-day in readiness to come to Camp 5 to-morrow. Soon Camp 4 was hidden by cloud. It rose, white and billowy, filling the Yalung and creeping over the Talung Saddle. To the west all was cloud: there, only the spire of Jannu soared above it.

That night Brown moved in with Band so that they could share a bottle of oxygen. Mather came into my tent. In bed, I turned on the radio: Hardie spoke from Camp 4; he and Streather had come up, and now, because of our day's delay at Camp 5 to recover, they were following at an interval of one day instead of two. Then Clegg relayed to us from Base the weather forecast: the monsoon was reported in the Arakan; in three days it would reach the Eastern Himalaya. We did not know whether we were counted as in the Eastern Himalaya, but we hoped not: we needed five good days.

We began to stir at a quarter to five. Camp 5 was in shadow until ten o'clock, and so always cold in the morning, even on fine days. Whatever the weather, the cold shadow, the wind and the showers of driven snow beating against the tents always before we came outside made the day seem a bad one. We had determined that however bad it seemed we would get ready, and not, as often pays in sites where the sun comes earlier, wait for its warmth to raise our spirits. Two hours went by while snow was melted for drinks. Slowly we emerged and put on our boots. We used to time this operation in order to have a record in figures of the time taken by such a simple act at different heights, with and without oxygen. This morning I took five minutes to put on each boot, and rested ten minutes between one boot and the other. At last they were on, and all our bulky warm clothing. We turned to assemble the oxygen sets, strapping on the cylinders for this day's use, and connecting to them the copper feed-pipes. We had to do this for the Sherpas, too, and then try the sets to see that there was no leak. The bottles and valves were cold, and as soon as we turned the taps, there was violent hissing as the gas leaked out. We must warm them up. Since there were several cylinders leaking we could not warm them with our hands: we melted more snow, warmed up the water, and poured it over the valves. It took time, but it worked. At last all was ready for the loads to be made up. Each of us tied some of the gear to his oxygen frame: there was a tent to go, two large bottles weighing sixteen pounds each, a small one of nine pounds, a stove, kerosene, and food. Indispensables such as matches, priming fuel for the stove, and spanners for the oxygen sets, were checked at the last minute, and we were ready to put on our crampons. For this, we knelt in the snow. The metal was cold, and if our hands were bare our fingers lost all feeling within a few seconds of touching it; in the slightest wind, feeling was lost at once even without touching the metal. We wore double-layer silk gloves for putting on crampons and for work on the oxygen sets, and they were good: the fingers lasted until the job was done. Numb fingers took a long time to regain feeling; exposure to cold for only a few seconds might mean a loss of

The upper slopes of the Yalung face

fifteen minutes. We were now ready, and we roped up. Mather and I were on each end of the first rope, Dawa Tenzing and Ang Norbu between us. We wanted to do all the trail-breaking and step-cutting, so that Band and Brown might be as fit as possible next day.

We turned the ice-cliff immediately above camp at its west end. At the top of the slope down which we had walked into camp there was an ice-slope about a hundred feet high, the top of which hid what lay immediately above. We found there a crevasse, crossed by a long stride, then gentler slopes of snow, the lowest slopes of the bay beneath the Sickle. There were a few small crevasses, but none looked wide; the surface of the snow was a dull white, varied by glistening patches which promised ice-crust and good going in crampons. We headed for the lowest rocks of the 'handle' of the Sickle; the snow was sometimes soft and sometimes crusty; the crust bore our weight, and we made good speed; our first rest was at the foot of the rocks.

There was here a hollow scooped out of the snow by the eddying wind: we hoped that somewhere high up the Gangway, where a ridge of rock stuck out of the snow, there might be a similar hollow scooped, a place for us to pitch the tent. The rock was rough, brownish-red and firm; we had not been near rock of any kind since leaving the Hump, where the rock was ugly, splintered and grey, and we had touched none since Base. We sat for ten minutes here, oxygen turned off. We had been going an hour, and already were near the foot of the Gangway.

Between us and the Gangway were a number of rock-bluffs separated by gullies filled with snow or ice. From a distance, and in photographs, this section had looked very steep and smooth, but now we found that the general angle was not much over forty-five degrees. Speed was our greatest need, and all depended on the quality of the snow between the rocks.

So far I had been leading; now Mather took the lead. We crossed a small bergschrund, and he started cutting steps up and across to the right, towards a promising funnel between the rocks. The slope was too hard for us to drive in the shafts of our axes, but the steps were in such good snow-ice that there was little danger. The chips from Mather's axe twirled down past me and, looking down, I saw them glancing over the unbroken rocks below before they disappeared in the direction of the wide icy shoot to the east of our camp. After some fifty yards Mather turned straight up, and we zig-zagged up a ribbon of snow a few yards wide. It was rather slow going, since the slope here was steeper, about fifty degrees, but progress was steady. The upper part of this gully looked more difficult and hid the Gangway above, but a tongue of snow led up to our right less steeply, and we followed it. Here I took a turn again, and found that the snow was less good; there was a surface slab two or three inches thick lying on a little soft snow; but we were able to tread a foothold in the layer under that, and in three-quarters of an hour from the bergschrund we at last reached the Gangway.

We were on a snow-field three hundred feet wide; before us it rose for fifteen hundred feet to the west ridge of the mountain. The snow on it was unbroken save that above us, where it abutted against the south-west face of the mountain, a few rocks showed.

The snow here was good: the top inch was a little soft and clogged the crampons, but with two or three scrapes it was possible to make a good step in the firm snow beneath. Climbing in Sola Khumbu, I had come to think that some of the best of all Himalayan snow is found on south-facing slopes, and here, too, the rule seemed to be true. By tradition these slopes, subject to heavy snowfall, exposed to the tropical sun which melts the snow on them to a great depth, are dangerous. Here the snow was all that we could wish for.

By now we were all excited. Dawa Tenzing, just behind me, pressed at my heels, urging me to let him go ahead and cut the steps. I did so, and our pace increased at once: cut, cut, step; cut, cut, step; we saw the peaks around us sink; the great Gangway lengthened beneath us, and the rocks under the west ridge, which make narrower its upper third, came closer. We had one rest, where some slabs stuck out of the snow half-way up the Gangway. We climbed over them, scraping away the snow above them to rest our loads: there were no proper ledges.

When we started again, Dawa Tenzing stayed in the lead, and our pace was as fast as before. Here a wide gully came down from the north-east to join the Gangway, and we headed away across the mouth of it, a long section on which the snow in places was less good: there were patches of slab-snow, some- times several inches thick, alternating with bare, glistening snow-ice. By one-thirty we had crossed the mouth of the gully and reached the rocks which border the narrower upper third of the Gangway. We had thought that somewhere here we might find a hollow scooped in the snow by wind at the edge of the rocks; but there was nothing. Where the snow joined the rocks there was merely a flattening, hard and icy, a foot wide, over which icicles several feet long hung from the cliffs above; below, the snow swept in an unbroken sheet down the Gang- way.

Ahead, barely sticking out of the snow, we saw rocks in the bed of the Gangway; somewhere there there might be a place for a camp; we headed for them; they were only two or three hundred feet away. The slope, which lower on the Gangway had been about forty degrees, was steeper here, and I began to notice that I was slowing up and breathing more quickly. My oxygen had come to an end; the pressure-gauge had been read- ing zero for some minutes already. Suddenly Dawa looked over his shoulder and said something about it being my turn to go in front. I knew that his oxygen, too, must have run out. On the Gangway he had given us a better pace than could have been set on that slope by any other of our party. I stepped past him. Here the snow was hard and smooth, without surface powder; the slope was of about fifty degrees, so that we could easily rest the inner hand on it. I was very slow indeed. I would cut a step, and then take anything up to twenty hard breaths before starting to cut the next, or making a step up. Half an hour later the rocks were only a few yards away. Upon the cutting of each step the mind had to be centred as upon the object of life: each in turn was the last thing I would ever have to do; then all ambition had to be transferred to the next, and to the next. At last my hands were on the lowest rocks; I stood there for minutes on end, head bowed, leaning on the rock, before I could drag myself onto a ledge a few inches wide, where I could sit while weakly hauling in the rope. One by one, we all reached the rocks and looked round. There was no place to camp; the rocks were hopeless, the snow hard and steep; I dropped an empty oxygen bottle and it shot away down the Gangway; it would not stop before the Great Shelf. Above us we saw nothing more promising, and it was past two o'clock. Besides, I doubt if one of us, without oxygen, could have gone another step. The camp had to be here.

We began to dig in the snow beside the rocks. It was painfully slow work: one Sherpa after another took a turn with his axe, and after a few scrapes lay exhausted, unable to move. I gathered in the oxygen sets, took off the empty cylinders and carefully wedged the loads on the small ledges. To lift a small oxygen cylinder weighing less than nine pounds demanded a concentrated effort of will.

Then Band found that his Sherpa, Tashi, still had an oxygen cylinder one-third full. At one of our halts, when we had all turned off our oxygen, Tashi must have forgotten to turn his on again: he had come part way without using it, and without betraying to anyone the fact that he was climbing without it.

Band now took Tashi's set, and began to dig with renewed strength. Gradually the ledge took shape, and in two hours it was ready for the tent. When bedrock was reached, the ledge was four and a half feet wide. The tent was six inches wider: when pitched, it was askew, its outer wall overhanging the slope, its guys tied to axes pushed into the snow above. It was cramped and exposed, but we could do no better. The height was about 26,900 feet.

It was now four o'clock, time for Mather and the Sherpas and me to start. First we had to rope up. We had climbed on two ropes, one of which we were leaving for Band and Brown; we had merely to tie on, Mather and I at each end, the four Sherpas spaced between us. It took fifteen minutes. Each had on his back an oxygen frame stripped of its load and of its empty cylinder; axes were sorted; Mather led; one by one the Sherpas followed, each pressing the hands of Band and Brown and wishing them good luck.

The first few steps were a relief, the downhill work seemed easy; but soon we realized that, tired as we were, even going downhill was exhausting. In less than a hundred yards we had stopped for our first rest, in fifty more for our second. The distances between stops became shorter, and lower down, where the snow in places was loose on the surface, we thought we did well to take fifty steps without stopping. The pace in front used to slacken until one of the leading figures slumped down in the snow; or the drag of the rope checked those ahead, and from the rear we called out, "A rest, a rest". These halts were not a brief pause, and then on; we sat or half lay, axe-shafts driven into the snow, every muscle relaxed, hoping for some return of strength. Minutes passed, until not returning strength, but the knowledge that we could not stay for ever here, stirred us to another effort, and one by one we would push ourselves to our feet.

By the time we reached the steep slopes at the bottom of the Gangway, one or other of us sank down in the snow every few yards. At each halt, when the slope allowed, the Sherpas lay full length. Between halts, we swayed from footstep to footstep. No thought was spared for the possible consequences of a slip. Fatigue dulls fear, and we even treated casually the slope of ice above Camp 5, which in the morning we had thought steep enough. Every thought was for finding strength to stand straight, to keep the back from doubling up, to step down.

Hardie and Streather had come up to-day with Urkien and Ila Tenzing from Camp 4, and when we reached the foot of the slope, they saw us and started up towards us. Streather led Mather to a box where he could sit; Hardie put his arm round the first of our Sherpas; the Sherpas moved into camp with a curious jerky gait, legs apart, unbending, like puppets in slow motion. All of them, even Dawa, lay flat on their backs in the snow, unmoving. Abruptly I sat down, and Hardie clapped an oxygen mask on my face. A few breaths worked wonders, and soon we were describing the day, and telling where the camp was. Urkien and Ila Tenzing came round filling our mugs, and slowly we revived. The plan had been that Mather should take Ang Norbu, Ang Dawa and Tashi down to Camp 4 to-day. This was now impossible; but fortunately there was room here for all; Mather and I shared our old tent, Hardie and Streather that used by Band and Brown. For a long time Neil Mather and I just lay there; the sun had set long since, and outside it was cold: during the day we had felt our strength, even our life, ebbing away; still they had not flowed back. Then all at once I dug Neil in the ribs, and shouted: "Neil, they're up there." For a few minutes we had a shouting match.

CHAPTER TWELVE

THE SUMMIT RIDGE

May 25th

WHEN we began our journey down to Camp 5, George Band and Joe Brown set about their preparations for the night. It was after four: the edge of the shadow cast by the cliffs of Kangchenjunga West was creeping near and soon would cut them off from the warmth of the sun, already feeble. They crawled into the tent, and George connected up the large oxygen cylinder that they were to share during the night; it was not quite full, but should last them about nine hours. Meanwhile, against the back of the ledge, Joe lit the Primus and began to melt snow. They wanted to eat as much as possible, and particularly to drink, for hard breathing in dry air robs the body of moisture very quickly. They made orangeade from crystals, and followed it up with sweet tea. Supper consisted of asparagus soup from a packet, lambs' tongues from a tin, and mashed potato. Then they drank again, this time chocolate, drinking it slowly in order to keep it down. It was a meal which they really enjoyed, an unusual experience at high camps. While they ate, the sun was sinking behind Jannu, throwing great golden rays through rents in the cloud. Joe sat by the open tent-sleeve, watching, and took photograph after photograph as the colours changed. "It was terrific," he says. George, inside the tent, was taking out a partly exposed reel of film so as to have a full reel for the morrow. He found his fingers clumsy: they were slightly frost-bitten, all the tips blistered. They had lost feeling that morning at Camp 5 while he was wearing only one pair of tattered silk gloves; and not realizing how cold it was he had worked a moment too long. At eight o'clock, when it was time to get into the sleeping-bags, the question arose who should sleep on the outside, where the tent sagged over the ledge. Joe broke two matchsticks and offered them; George chose the shorter, and lost. They felt so precariously perched that they tied on the rope and George made it fast to a spike of rock on the slabs close to the tent. Outside, he took a last look round; there were two levels of cloud to be seen, the lower a layer of settled cumulus, the upper murky and thunderous. Threads of lightning flickered over the plains. On the mountain it was absolutely still.

As they lay side by side, fragments of snow kept skittering down the slope and bombarding the tent. Occasional eddies of wind rustled the canvas, and these, together with the pattering from above, suggested to George's anoxic, sleep-befuddled mind that new snow was falling; but luckily it was a fine night, and inside the tent they were reasonably warm. To cut down weight they had brought only their outer sleeping-bags, and inside them they wore every scrap of clothing they had, even their boots. George at this time, afraid that if he took off his boots they would be frozen hard, wore them continuously for three days and three nights.

Sleep did not come easily, kept off, perhaps, partly by excitement. Soon after turning on the oxygen they felt warmth flooding through their chilled limbs down to their toes. To George, the suck and swish of each breath against the soft rubber mask seemed like the surge and wash of waves on a dark sea-shore. He had come to expect, in the first few minutes after donning his mask at night, grotesque highly coloured dreams; but this night the colours were drab.

When the oxygen finished, soon after five o'clock, they woke at once. Balancing the Primus between them, they began melting snow, and in three hours had produced water enough to have two mugs of tea each and to fill a flask with lemonade for the coming day; they ate only some biscuits. At eight-fifteen they started. The tent was still in shade but the west side of the Gangway was lit by the sun, and as they climbed they bore to the left to meet it. At first George led. The snow was hard, and for a few steps he thought that they could climb in their crampons without cutting; then, remembering that on the way down they would be very tired, he began to cut steps.

We had studied this last part of the climb through binoculars from Base Camp, and although we had at one time proposed to climb the Gangway as far as the west ridge and follow that ridge towards the top, this plan had been discarded in favour of following a line of snow-patches and broken rocks which we had seen on the south-west face. Starting about two hundred feet below the west col, this line sloped up across the face towards the foot of a snowy spur which ran up to join the west ridge between the summit and a cluster of prominent rock-pinnacles.

As they climbed step by step up the Gangway, under the great cliffs of its east wall, it was hard to know which snow-patch marked the start of their intended traverse. George lifted his mask to make himself heard and called, "Do you think that's it, Joe?" "Perhaps. Let's look." Neither was sure, and George cut up and round a steep corner. There was more snow and rock ahead, and still they could not see enough to be sure. For an hour George cut up snow and over ice-glazed rock. Then they rounded another corner and saw before them a sheer wall of brown rock about two hundred feet high, broken only by successive lines of overhang. It was, Joe says, "VS stuff"—'Very Severe'—and they retraced their steps to the Gangway.

The mistake had cost them an hour and a half, in time and in oxygen. They now shared the lead, and continued up the Gangway, making for its eastern fork, keeping to the right of a tall rock-pinnacle. They cut in zig-zags, wielding the axe one-handed; slash, slash, step; slash, slash, step; they moved quickly.

The west ridge from the air

Above the fork of the Gangway the cliffs to their right grew less steep, and there, sparkling in the sun, they saw their snow-patches, which this time there was no mistaking; but above, in shade, there were still steep rocks through which they saw no obvious break. Turning off the Gangway, they found slabby rocks, and gullies and ledges covered with snow. To Joe it was natural to turn at once to the rocks; but some of the low walls were harder than they had looked and in places George preferred the snow. Soon they took off their crampons and tied them to their packs. They had taken off their canvas overboots the night before, and now, for the first time since Base Camp, their rubber soles gripped the bare rock. Presently they reached steeper rock, a forty-foot buttress, brown, rough and easy. Above it was snow with a slabby crust, which felt as if it might break away under them; it led to more rock, and here for safety Joe put in a peg to which to fasten the rope. He swung round a corner to the right; for a moment he was hanging from his hands, his feet dangling; then he entered a chimney in which there was ice, climbed it, and traversed to the right again across a slabby face. Here it was airy, but the holds, Joe says, were good: "A really nice position." When George followed, he thought that the hardest part was the move just above the ice-filled chimney, up a little slab where there were no holds except a crack on the left. The exposed traverse led to the foot of an ice-gully. It was a hundred and twenty feet long, and steep, about sixty degrees: as Joe cut up it, he could rest his side against the steps. They climbed it in two pitches; half-way, there was a small rocky nose which they used as a halting-place. Joe for the first time was beginning to feel tired, and George tried to summon up the energy to take over the lead; but it was clear that Joe was getting the more benefit from his oxygen, and they decided that he should continue. George belayed his rope round an axe stuck between ice and rock while Joe slowly cut up the rest of the gully. There was little room on the stance

The final crack

and the belay was poor: it felt like a perch in mid-air above the Great Shelf and the Yalung. At the top of the gully the snow petered out between constricting rock walls and they climbed out with a twist of the body. They had reached the crest of the snowy spur which led to the west ridge above the cluster of pinnacles, and for the first time could see the rocks under the summit. The distance to the main ridge was only about fifty yards, the slope here of only about thirty degrees; they were tempted to stop cutting and to climb it in crampons, but thought it better to be cautious, and continued to cut steps, moving together, slowly. They had been going continuously for five hours, and George felt his throat parched and clots of phlegm sticking to the roof of his mouth. Once or twice, he saw that Joe's goggles were pushed up on his forehead, and called to warn him, but the sun did not seem bright, and the misty goggles were a continual nuisance; for half the day Joe's eyes went unprotected.

So far they had felt no wind; now, reaching the crest of the main ridge, they found a fresh breeze blowing from the northwest, carrying flurries of snow above their heads. On the very crest they found shelter in a small hollow, a natural balcony enclosed on three sides by a wall of ice about three feet high and a foot thick; there they sat down to eat; it was their first rest. The cluster of pinnacles was just below them; beyond it they saw Kangchenjunga West, and beyond that a layer of cloud. They could see far down the north side, and though it did not look as if the north ridge could be climbed straight up from the north col, it looked as if from the col the north face could be traversed, to reach the west ridge where they now sat. Looking back the way they had come, they saw rocks at the lower end of the snowy spur, then nothing until the Great Shelf. It was a glorious place, but they could not linger to enjoy it. Time was pressing. It was two o'clock, and they had only two hours' supply of oxygen left. George said that they must turn back by three or risk a night out. "In that case," Joe answered, "we've got to be there by three."

After ten minutes they started again. "From then on," Joe says, "it was a ridge like Crib Gôch—easy scrambling rocks—with snow and ice on it; that was just in the hollows where you put your feet; everything you got hold of was clean, the rocks where they stuck out dry and clean." Ahead the slope of the ridge was gentle at first, then rose abruptly, a tower of brown and grey rock sixty feet high. They moved together for about a rope's-length at or near the very crest before taking to the south side of the ridge for a further rope's-length. Joe, who was still in the lead, was using John Clegg's axe this day, his own having broken earlier in the expedition; it had a sling which he found convenient for dangling it from his wrist when using both hands on the rock; he also carried, tied to his pack, a small axe like a piton-hammer for use in very steep places. George, because of the clumsiness of his frost-bitten hands, found that it was very difficult to manage rope and axe, let alone grasp the rock.

The traverse brought them to a gully of rocks and snow which finished sixty feet up against a sheer wall; at that point there was a large block wedged in the gully, and George, when he came up, anchored himself while Joe examined the wall ahead. The rock was rough and dry, golden-brown in sunshine. There was more than one crack running up it; Joe picked the likeliest, one at the back of a recess; at its foot were some square-cut blocks, which he reached by a short traverse across snow-covered ledges. The place was exposed; below were the cliffs up to which they had looked earlier when they had lost the route on the Gangway; "If you came off the crack," Joe says, "you wouldn't have to bounce much before you were going down very steep rocks." He fixed a runner,[1] and started. The crack was one which low down he could have climbed with

[1] Runner—a 'running belay' made by threading the climber's rope through a ring fixed to the mountain. See Colour Plate 6, facing p. 124.

ease, but here he wondered for how long he would have the strength to hang by his hands, and he turned his oxygen to the full six litres a minute. Two moves brought him to a chock-stone to which he fastened a second runner; above, some blocks formed an overhang; though their edges offered a good grip, they looked insecure, and he preferred to jam his fists in the cracks at their sides; he pulled up and round the bulge, to the right.

George, watching, had no inkling of what lay beyond, till suddenly Joe, at the top of the wall, turned his head and shouted, "George, we're there." A few minutes later, George himself had climbed the crack. Where they stood, some huge flat slabs of grey rock made a platform; before them rose a cone of snow, about twenty feet away and a few feet higher than the place where they stood; it was the top.

A few feet to their right was another flat rock-table; it was on the south side of the top, and here they went to take photographs with the top as background. Of the view, except to the north-east, where it was cut off by the top, they took a complete panorama. Sikkim and Darjeeling were hidden under a bubbling sea of cloud which flowed round the south ridge of the mountain and spread towards the plains. They could see Camps 4 and 2, black specks: the cloud-level was at about 20,000 feet. Far off, only the highest peaks stood above it, like rocky islands lapped by waves: Makalu and Chomolonzo, Lhotse and Everest.

From the south ridge, Joe looked down the east face but could see only cloud; then he walked to the west ridge and made fast George's rope round his short axe stuck in the snow so that George could join him. They looked down the slabs of the north ridge and saw on one side the top of Bauer's spur, and on the other the grey snake of the Kangchenjunga glacier. Tibet was only thirteen miles away, and beyond the savage outlines of the Twins and Nepal Peak they could see its rolling uplands, dry and dun-coloured, half hidden by cloud, only streaked with snow.

George says that a lot of people have asked him: "Wasn't there a great temptation to go those last few feet?"; and that the answer is no. "For one thing," he says, "I was too tired to want to take another step. But apart from that, I'm glad we left no footmark on the top." I think that we all felt the same. Had it not been for our promise, we should have gone to the top, without doubt; but as it was, keeping the promise cost us no regret. The gesture seemed fitting enough.

It was late, and cloud was coming up, and after fifteen minutes, at three o'clock, they started down, each taking with him a piece of rock, speckled grey and black gneiss, which later could be cut or broken into smaller pieces. For a moment they wondered if they should lower themselves down the highest crack on a doubled rope; then they decided to climb down it. They did not find it so difficult as on the way up. Joe left there the sling round the chockstone, in case Norman Hardie and Tony Streather should want to make use of it. Their first stop after that was at the balcony above the cluster of pinnacles, where they ate some mint cake, and finished their lemon drink, leaving their flask on the ridge.

Near the bottom of the snowy spur Joe began to gasp, as if, he says, he was doing some really hard work: his oxygen was finished. He took off the set and dumped it on the snow. A short way below, in the gully which had led them up to the snow-ridge, George's also finished, and his set was dumped near the stance half-way up the gully, where Norman Hardie photographed it next day. When they went on, they were slower, and stopped often for short rests; not far above the Gangway they put on the crampons which for most of the day they had carried; they felt very tired.

They were now in shadow, the light of the sunset glowing on the crags above them, and when at last they reached the upper part of the Gangway it was beginning to grow dark. It was difficult to see the steps, and in places new steps had to be cut: on the way up they had cut their steps rather far apart. Once or twice they thought they heard a whistle or call from below, and Joe whistled in reply. It seemed much farther down the Gangway than up, and, Joe says, "We didn't see the tent till we were right on it. We never thought we weren't going to reach it, but we had begun to wonder just when." It was dark by now, seven o'clock; Norman Hardie and Tony Streather were inside, and the Primus was purring. "Did you make it?" They grunted in reply and sank down on the snow at the tent door. Never had they felt so thirsty.

CHAPTER THIRTEEN

THE SUMMIT RIDGE

May 26th

ON May 19th Norman Hardie and Tony Streather had been left at Camp 3; with them were Urkien and Ila Tenzing, who were later to go with them to Camp 6. During the day, Streather chose food for their top camp, and Hardie checked over the oxygen equipment. One of the open-circuit sets had a faulty flow-regulator, and he changed it for a regulator from a closed-circuit set, a small change, but one which had an important effect on their final climb: the new regulator allowed a smaller rate of flow than was ordinarily possible in the open-circuit set, and when later, near the top, they found themselves very short of oxygen, they were able to make what they had last longer. Towards nightfall the Sherpas who had been that day to Camp 5 arrived. Their return was a tonic to the four at Camp 3: someone was certain now to climb far above the ledge where to-day the loads had been left. The Sherpas were near exhaustion. For two and a half days one of them, Gyalgen, lay just inside the door of Norman Hardie's tent. Twice he drank a mug of soup; otherwise, in all that time, Norman never saw him move.

The next two days were anxious ones at Camp 3 because Norman Hardie was now ill with bronchitis. He had suffered more than any one else from the usual high-altitude throat and cough; but now he was so much worse that he and Tony Streather began to fear that he might be unable to go higher. On the night of the 20th he was especially bad, lying awake coughing and gasping for breath until five in the morning, when he tried breathing oxygen; this partly relieved him, and he was able to sleep a little. Fortunately for him, all our moves were now delayed by the blizzard, and this gave him a chance to recover. On May 21st Jackson and MacKinnon came down from Camp 4 and helped to nurse him, and next morning I said over the radio that we were about to start for Camp 5 but that Hardie and Streather should stay one more day at Camp 3. That night and the next morning when they called us on the radio there was no reply; so they started up, hoping that my party was now safely at Camp 5.

As far as Camp 4 Hardie used a closed-circuit oxygen set, partly because the warm moist air breathed in this set would help his bronchitis and partly for the sake of giving the set one more test. Streather used an open-circuit set and led all the way. With them were Urkien and Ila Tenzing, and three other Sherpas who came for the day to give them a lift.

That night they were relieved to hear Camp 5 on the air. The radio had been recovered, but the news of avalanche losses was bad. All the oxygen meant for their party was lost; could they bring up more? Tony, listening over Norman's shoulder, said, "We can carry a ton." There was food to bring up also, and when they made up their loads in the morning there was more than two hundred pounds to carry. Toiling up the Shelf, Norman wished he had not brought the heavier closed-circuit apparatus, and when the soda-lime which absorbs carbon dioxide in the set was finished, tried to convert the apparatus into an open-circuit set, but without success. He seemed to go as fast without it, so he threw away the heavy mask and tubes and continued on what little oxygen there is in the air at 25,000 feet. They were cheered by seeing the Camp 6 party far up the Gangway; we were making good speed; Camp 6 was going to be high.

After a while Norman took Tony's set and changed places with him, breaking trail while Tony, who had been twice to this height without oxygen, ploughed in the rear and told him, between gasps, how good it was to breathe 'fresh air—none of that canned stuff'. On top of their oxygen frames were personal kit, clothes and bedding; the Sherpas, without oxygen and without complaint, carried even heavier loads. Shortly before the return of my party from above, they reached Camp 5 and settled in.

On the morning of May 25th they found the journey to Camp 6 fairly easy: all four breathed oxygen, and faint steps were visible where we had cut them; they needed no vicious swing of the axe, but only a gentle scrape to make them into a sound stairway. As they reached the tent, which George Band and Joe Brown for safety had collapsed before they left it that morning, Ila Tenzing said that his oxygen was finished. They set up the tent and had hot drinks all round.

We had hoped that the first pair would be down in time to return with the two Sherpas to Camp 5, though we were uncertain whether it would be a case of climbers escorting weary Sherpas or of Sherpas escorting weary climbers; but at four o'clock there was still no sign of the first pair, and the Sherpas started down. Norman and Tony watched anxiously: the slope was steep, and there was no oxygen for climbers coming down from Camp 6. But they need not have worried: they had parted from two very capable men, who when they reached us at Camp 5 were still comparatively fresh.

At five o'clock Norman and Tony began to worry about George and Joe. A little earlier, they had only been rueful at the prospect of a crowded night, four in a tent made for two; but this feeling soon gave way to increasing concern for the safety of the others. At five-thirty the sun left the tent, and the temperature dropped suddenly. The oxygen of the first pair must have been finished some time since, and there was not long till dark. Norman and Tony waited anxiously. Then, when it was already quite dark, there was a shout; I heard it,

29 Looking south from the highest point   Kangchenjunga II

30 *Top* Below the snowy spur   Streather on May 26th. '*an ice gully. It was a hundred and twenty f...
long, and steep*'

Bottom At the foot of the last rocks   Band on May 25th. '*traverse brought them to a gully of rocks and sno...*

The view west   Chamlang, Makalu, Lhotse, Everest

32 The view north   The North-east Spur, The Twins, Nepal Peak and Tent Pea

too, from Camp 5, and went out with a torch in the starlight. George and Joe were high on the Gangway. Norman and Tony answered, and not long after welcomed the others, with great relief. George and Joe sank down on the snow-ledge by the tent door, and did not move till they had had hot drinks.

All now crowded into the tent and prepared for the night. They arranged themselves fanwise, their legs bunched in a corner, like, George says, the stalks of a handful of flowers. There were sleeping-bags and oxygen only for two, and Nor-man and Tony had these. George and Joe were still roped, but this time forgot to hook the rope over a rock outside. George again had the outer edge of the tent, and lay in the overhanging sag of the canvas; it creaked whenever he moved, and he hoped that the stitching was strong. He remembers no wink of sleep. He wriggled his toes in his boots to help the circulation, and every little while looked at the luminous dial of his watch as it ticked the minutes away. Joe's eyes, which soon after he reached camp had begun to prick, were burning. He was wedged be-tween two Lilos, lying only on the groundsheet, but he felt no cold: his mind was occupied by his pain, which steadily increased, and seemed to him worse than the pain he had once felt when lime had dropped into his eyes. All night he turned over and over, over and over. Norman and Tony, trying to rest as best they could, in wakeful moments plied the others with questions about the route. Where on each pitch were the pitons? What was the snow like? How difficult were the rocks? When and where had they taken off their crampons? For the four, talking and dozing on the narrow ledge at 27,000 feet, the night was long. At last day broke, again fair. At five they lit the stove, but it was more than three hours before anyone was ready to move. In spite of Joe's eyes, George's frost-bitten finger-tips, and the night's discomfort, all were in good spirits. They ate and drank a little, and George and Joe started down; Norman and Tony, after assembling their oxygen sets, and checking the fastening of their spare cylinders, were off at eight-thirty.

When they had made their plans for this last climb they had decided that, in addition to the large 1,600-litre oxygen cylinder carried by each of the first pair, they would each carry also a small 800-litre cylinder. If the other two in fine weather failed to climb the final ridge, assuming that it could be climbed, it was likely to be either because of a mistake in the route or because of lack of time; the extra oxygen would give them a greater range, and the experience of the first pair might help them to a better route. Now each had with him 2,400 litres of oxygen instead of the 1,600 litres each taken by George and Joe. They started by using the small cylinders.

On the Gangway they found some of the steps of yesterday, filled with loose snow which had to be scraped out; for most of the way new steps had to be cut. The angle was almost gentle enough for them to climb the slope in crampons without making steps, and the snow was firm; they led alternately, and when Tony was in the lead his mind, he says, was all the time occupied with the problem, "Is it worth cutting another step, or shall I trust to my crampons?" They played safe, as George and Joe had done, and the steps were cut; progress, nevertheless, was fast, and in less than two hours they had turned off the Gangway onto the south-west face. Here Tony called to Norman that his windproof, strapped on top of his oxygen frame, was loose. Norman swung the frame off his back to make fast the windproof, and his large oxygen cylinder slipped out of the straps. Touching the ice, its valve was struck, and Tony could hear the oxygen hissing out as the cylinder passed close by him and vanished. A third of their supply of oxygen was gone. Saying nothing, Norman turned his oxygen off and climbed for two rope's-lengths without it, going very slowly. Then Tony came up to him and said, "Use my large cylinder, and I'll get along with the two small ones." Tony's regulator happened to be the one with the extra low flow-rate, and if he turned it to its lowest flow, while Norman cut the steps, things would be about equal. It was a sound plan, and they changed bottles and went on.

To the west ridge they followed the route taken by the first pair, except at one place where Norman chose a snow-gully rather than climb some rocks. They thought the hardest place was a slabby rock-pitch which they reached not long after leaving the Gangway, and it was here, on the descent, that they put in a piton. As they climbed up towards the ridge, the cluster of pinnacles, says Tony, seemed to hang over them: the tallest was a hundred feet high, its sheer rocks brown, its face smooth and cut by vertical cracks. Preferring ice to rock, along the west ridge they kept below the crest on the south side, following a line a little lower than that taken by George and Joe. Here they were completely sheltered from the wind, which blew strongly over the ridge above them. They were in sunshine and felt uncomfortably warm in their eiderdown suits. There was an unbroken bed of cloud at 20,000 feet, but around them and above there was none. Once they saw figures, minute specks, on the Great Shelf: probably the first pair on their way down to Camp 4. Since leaving the Gangway they had had only one short rest, and although they were moving fast and had their oxygen turned low, they had thoroughly enjoyed the climbing: the world was below them, and they felt no longer a part of it.

They recognized at once Joe's route up the last rock-wall, and scouted round for some alternative: for one thing they preferred, if they could, to finish the climb without taking off their crampons; for another, they hoped to dispense with the use of the rope-sling left by the first pair. Tony waited at the foot of the crack while Norman looked farther to the right. Round a corner he found a snow-ramp; they followed it and reached the south ridge of the mountain about a hundred feet from the top. To the platform on the Nepal side reached by George and Joe was a plain walk, and they rejoined the other route at the top of the crack. A few moments earlier, it had seemed to them that they were still far from the top: to them, as to the first pair, the end was abrupt, something of a surprise.

It was only twelve-fifteen; the climb had taken a little under four hours; in every direction it was clear, and the wind had dropped; they still felt fresh; they thought that the climb down would be quick, and that they could reach Camp 5 easily by nightfall. They settled down to enjoy themselves, in no hurry to cut short a time of unique delight. They took photographs, and sat chatting and eating; they found that here they had a better appetite than at Camp 6. While Tony changed his oxygen cylinder, Norman went to a gap in the west ridge from which he could look down to the north; the top of the north-east spur seemed unexpectedly far off, and the ridge dropping to it steep and hard. Beyond it, past the Twins and Nepal Peak, were the brown hills of Tibet. He looked long at Makalu; we did not then know that it had already been climbed; next year, perhaps, he might be there himself; he thought of Franco's party on the mountain and wished them the good fortune that we had had.

Fifty-five happy minutes passed quickly. They left on the snow an empty small cylinder, and Tony led off down.

For a short way all was well; then Norman saw Tony going off the track. He seemed to be uncertain where he was, and was moving all at once with extreme slowness and heavy effort. Norman went down to him: his goggles were fogged so that he could not see, and his oxygen cylinder, which had been re-opened only a few minutes, was empty. Some unnoticed leak during the day had deprived them of nearly the whole of its contents, and for the descent they now had only what was left in Norman's large cylinder, about one-third full.

Tony suggested that Norman, as the more experienced,

should come down last, and, using what oxygen was left, safe-guard the two of them.

Progress now was very slow indeed. Before leaving the west ridge they stopped a moment for Tony to take a few breaths from Norman's oxygen mask. Not far from the Gangway they came down the only difficult rocks they had climbed, and here Norman drove in a piton for support in case of a slip. Even on the Gangway they could not move down easily: their steps had filled with snow, and every one had carefully to be scraped clear before it could be used. They reached Camp 6 at five o'clock.

CHAPTER FOURTEEN

RETURN

CAMP 5 was our link between the four above and the main body of the expedition below. On May 25th the hours passed slowly. Clegg, watching from Base through glasses, told us on the radio that the first pair had left Camp 6 at eight o'clock. Hardie and Streather left us soon after, with Urkien and Ila Tenzing. I saw Mather off down, with Ang Norbu, Tashi and Ang Temba; Dawa and I waited. We could see nothing from our camp of what went on higher up, and Clegg, watching from Base, had news only that one of the Sherpas at Base had been taken ill; cloud hid the mountain from him. The sick man was Pemi Dorje, who had been exhausted after the carry to Camp 5 on May 19th; he had seemed to recover on the way down, but after reaching Base he had become partly paralysed, and was now unconscious. The afternoon was still and warm; Dawa and I sat outside, looking over the sea of cloud. The radio calls were unvaried: Pemi Dorje was much the same; from above there was no sign. About two o'clock Jackson, MacKinnon, Annullu, Kunde Ang Dawa, and Pasang Sonar arrived without oxygen, bringing stores; each was making the journey to this camp for the second time. They crowded into my tent for a drink and a rest, and described how, from the Shelf, they had watched Band and Brown leave Camp 6 and go up the Gangway until, on the rocks, they had lost sight of them. At four they started down, and at a quarter past five Urkien and Ila Tenzing returned, reporting that they had made good time to Camp 6, that all was well there, and that they had seen nothing of the first pair. Soon after, Jackson

138

spoke on the radio from Camp 4: the first pair ought now to be on their way down from Camp 6, but he had a clear view of the upper slopes of the mountain and could see no one.

The sun set, and the cold came, as always, in a few moments. We struggled into our bags as light began to fail. I went out and called a few times; there was no reply. At nearly seven Ila Tenzing suddenly said, "Listen". He thought he had heard someone call. We dressed and went out. It was dark but for the faint glow of starlight on the snow, and cold. We stood listening, ears strained; not a sound. I went to the foot of the ice-slope, and heard a call far off, faint and indistinct; Ila Tenzing heard it too, and came towards me with a torch. We both shouted, and thought we heard an answer; but if it was an answer it was not repeated, though we shouted again, several times. It was evident that whatever had happened today, the first pair were not close above us, and we returned to the tents. Not until morning did we hear, by radio from MacKinnon, that they were on their way down to us.

They reached us at nine, and rested till twelve, when they started down with Urkien. The rest had done them good, but they were still shaky. Joe Brown was partially snow-blind.

We called John Clegg at Base to tell him of the first pair's success. Throughout the day, he and I spoke to each other every hour; Pemi Dorje was worse, and soon after midday he died. This was sad news for us all. For Dawa Tenzing in particular it was a great grief: he was Pemi Dorje's brother-in-law; he had thought much of him, and had chosen him for the expedition.

We busied ourselves with small jobs around camp, and in the late afternoon we again sat outside; it was again warm and still; the clouds built themselves up like great snowy castles; sometimes, looking past Jannu at the setting sun, it was hard to tell what was cloud and what was mountain range. Jackson, who had come up a third time to Camp 4, bringing drops for

Brown's eyes, at four o'clock told me that he had seen the second pair return to Camp 6. I half expected them to come on down, but the hours passed, and they stayed in their tent. They were there for the night.

I was up and out at seven, looking for movement below the highest camp; there was none. It was a beautiful morning, the sun shining on a sea of cloud out of which rose only Kabru and Jannu, but it was very cold, and I went back to my bag.

At nine, I heard on the radio from John Jackson that Norman Hardie and Tony Streather had just started. I gave them half an hour, and then made my way to the foot of the ice-slope above camp, and up it; at its crest, I sat on the edge of the big crevasse there. Norman and Tony were above the narrows at the bottom of the Gangway, starting down the snow-gully between the rocks. I called to Dawa to bring up something for them to drink. He appeared at the foot of the slope, a water-bottle clutched in one hand, the shaft of his ice-axe in the other. He had always been the one to break the trail, to forge ahead when everyone else was exhausted, to try this and that way while we rested until he had found the best; he had been the one to carry our spare clothes, lightening our packs; now his lined face was tired, his step a slow haul from one foothold to the next, and he paused long between steps. We had no rope, and sat in the snow, waiting. When the two were within shouting distance, I called, "Are you all right?" "Yes, but we have to go slow." They came stiffly, a step at a time, swaying from the track, arms hanging, the rope idly trailing. Together we came into camp. Tony was blue, and barely able to stand: he had come down the whole way without oxygen. We had two bottles of it, nearly full, and gave him one to breathe. In a few minutes it revived him, and he was able to eat and drink a little.

After an hour's rest we came down to Camp 4. We had many stops on the way, but reached it in an hour. It was wind-swept as ever, the tents looking like wind-tunnels on the smooth slope, the snow packed, fine dust of snow sweeping gustily past. It was perhaps the finest viewpoint on the whole route, but it was never comfortable. John Jackson was there, and his Sherpas were able to lighten our loads. We went on. I came last, with Norman Hardie and Tony Streather. We did not hurry: we could not. It was a lovely evening, and the Upper Icefall was bright in the late sunshine. Before us was the great face of Kangchenjunga West, its fluted coat of ice green-blue and glistening, the ridges thrown into bold relief by the slanting light, the grooves in shadow. Beautiful though it was, we wished that each step was the last. At Camp 3 we sat on boxes outside the tents, watching Jannu and the clouds beneath us, drinking mugs of lemonade and eating hard army biscuits; after the sweet biscuits on which we had been largely living for the last few days, these plain biscuits seemed a luxury. Then we settled to sleep. Here we were under 22,000 feet, and feeling better.

There was still valuable equipment on the mountain. We left it there. What we could, tents and bedding, we brought; but at this season to have stayed any longer on the route above Base would have been to risk lives, and by the afternoon of May 28th everyone had reached Pache's Grave. It was none too soon. The snow in the Lower Icefall was softening everywhere, and the bergschrund east of the Hump was gaping. The ladder that had replaced the first firm bridge of snow now only just reached from lip to lip. West of the Hump, our daily passage had packed the route into a solid causeway several inches high, on either side of which the snow was soft and deep. The ice-ledge by which we had traversed the wall above the crevasse near Camp 1 had collapsed, and had to be re-cut; below Camp 1 an ice-avalanche had fallen across the track.

To Base too, spring had come. The snow had all gone; among the rough red boulders the mosses were tender and alive. Above the camp was the fresh earth where that morning Pemi Dorje had been buried under a great flat stone; all day the Sherpas were carving on it his name and the date, and 'Om Mani Padme Hum'; from the boulder against which Thondup had built his kitchen fluttered a bunch of prayer-flags tied to willow sticks. We missed Pemi Dorje. Usually untidy, his pigtail uncared-for, his locks about his face, he was always ready to grin, always ready to pick up his load; for steep and awkward places he had a natural aptitude; on the lift to Camp 5 he had passed the limit of his endurance in order to do his work. The Sherpas are a light-hearted people, and pass quickly from mood to mood. Soon they were laughing again, and it might have seemed to a stranger that, except by Dawa Tenzing and Tashi, Pemi Dorje was forgotten. But it was not so, and to talk to any of them about him was to recall their affection for him, and their sadness.

In two days we moved down to Moraine, reaching it in a day. There we rested, while coolies for the return journey were engaged at Ghunsa. On the meadow we pitched every tent and tarpaulin we had, making a great, gipsy-like encampment.

On the first night we had a camp-fire in the open. There was plenty of fuel now, and we sat round, piling on the logs to make a blaze. Over us was a thin film of cloud, hiding the mountain, the same roof of cloud upon which, night after night, we had looked down from Camp 3, Camp 4, and Camp 5, hiding the depths of the Yalung. For a moment the veil parted a little, and in the last of the light we saw faintly the Sickle and the Gangway, and above them, still untrodden, the summit; then the rift closed again.

For the first few days we were very tired. We were thin: when we stripped, we saw each other's ribs sticking out, and the muscles of our arms and shoulders were wasted; when we shaved, we saw faces so much shrunken that they seemed strange. We lay in the sun, and at night slept long and heavily.

After two days the Sherpas produced the expedition rugger-ball. Games often started, but they never lasted long: after five minutes half the players lay flat on the ground, panting.

About the same time the Sherpas began to dance in the evenings. The haunting, sweet songs are irresistible, and one by one we used to slip out of our tents in the dark to join the semicircle of dancers. As a rule they danced round a fire, and on our last night there they jammed open the valves of two canisters of butane gas and put a match to the gas as it came out. There was a roar, and a jet of flame that burnt fiercely and steadily, lighting up the whole camp. The dancers gathered round, tempted close as the flame sank, starting excitedly back when it suddenly flared again. It was a good ending.

On June 6th we broke camp, and began the journey home in pouring rain. Our old camp-site by the ruined temple was green and lush, an unkempt kitchen-garden, dock and rank weeds everywhere. The walk followed the usual pattern of Himalayan travel in the monsoon: rain, mist and drizzle; stony hillsides patched with dwarf rhododendron stretching up into cloud; the climb to passes half-seen; glimpses at evening when the cloud parted, opening sometimes vertically to show a great valley below us, sometimes horizontally, so that we saw in a frame slope beyond slope of wooded mountain-side, without top or bottom. We trudged along under our umbrellas.

On the second day we were to cross two passes. At the top of the first we lost the path on a wide stony plateau. We climbed a face seamed with grassy gullies to the wrong col, and beyond it found ourselves in a narrow valley whose V-shaped bottom was filled with great moss-covered boulders. We went down to the edge of the cloud, and saw below us the valley plunging down into rhododendron-thicket heavy with yellow bloom. It looked about knee-high, but Thondup, who was acting as guide, said it was head-high, and without a path impenetrable. Then we consulted the compass and found that we were going

143

west instead of east. The porters were somewhere ahead, on the right track, and we were without tents and bedding. There was nothing for it but to spend the night in the rain under our umbrellas. Fortunately we had a bag of rice, but it took three hours to make a fire. Next morning we retraced our steps. It took two days' hurried marching before we overtook our porters, who thought that we had wandered into the wilds of Nepal.

For the next five days we followed a good track along the crest of the Singalila. It is renowned for its views; we did not see them, but all the same it is a fine way to come back. It is high and cool, with plentiful flowers, rhododendrons, yellow, white and red, and carpets of blue primulas, and there are no leeches, and no people, except a few hospitable shepherds.

On June 13th we reached Tanglu, where Jack and Jill Henderson had come to meet us; with them was Tenzing Norkey, and others of our old friends among the Darjeeling Sherpas. By nightfall we were once more at Rungneet.

CHAPTER FIFTEEN

CONCLUSION

IN the last few years, seven of the world's highest mountains have been climbed. The reasons are the accumulation of knowledge, both of climbing at great heights and of individual mountains, and the development of equipment. To-day, we climb in down suits and light windproofs, wear well insulated boots, sleep on air-mattresses in warm bags, and use oxygen sets both by day and by night; and when we think of the men of the early expeditions, in their tweed jackets and knee-length puttees, felt hats, scarves and shooting-boots, and remember that without oxygen sets they carried camps as high as our highest, and climbed to a height about equal to that of Kangchenjunga, we are filled with respect.

It is the use of oxygen which, above all, has made the difference. This has made it possible to live high, yet continue to climb with vigour; men are less dependent now on their individual capacity to do with little oxygen; speed of climbing is increased, so that camps can be set farther apart and farther from the summit; Sherpas use oxygen to climb to the highest camps. It was the use of oxygen that made Everest possible; it played its part in Jean Franco's wonderful achievement on Makalu, when nine members of his expedition reached the summit; and on Kangchenjunga it made the final stages swifter and more sure.

Mountaineers have sometimes debated the rival merits of the large sponsored expedition, lavishly supplied, where the atmosphere is likely to be rather formal, and of the small, frugal expedition of three or four who know each other well. On Kangchenjunga it seemed to us that we had the best of both.

Through the hard work and generosity of our helpers at home we started with everything that we thought we really needed; and long before we set up our camp at Pache's Grave we had become a group of close friends.

Our Sherpas were straight from the mountains. They had been chosen by Dawa Tenzing, and he had made few mistakes. They were the kind of men who carried for the first Everest expeditions, trapesing ragged and wild over the 19,000-foot Nangpa La to see what was happening at Rongbuk, much as the Ghunsa men had come trotting into our early camp by the ruined temple. They were men to whom it was important to see the work done. They were, by their standards, well paid, and they were given a small bonus for carrying to the highest camps; but what took them there was pride. Good Sherpas are proud men, and what they will not do for its own sake, or for yours, they will not do for money.

It would be naïve to suppose that they can never change. Except those of the strongest character, it is unlikely that they can be proof against the great growth of Himalayan travel, and the penetration into the remotest places of caravans whose assumption is that it is money that matters. We are lucky to have enjoyed their friendship in days when they have not yet been much exposed to the chance of harm.

In the weather we were neither particularly lucky nor particularly unlucky. For the time of year, it was what was to be expected. In April and early May we had wind, and regular afternoon falls of snow. At a time when we much wanted fine weather we were storm-bound for two days, but were able to ride out the storm; and later, when the highest camp was occupied, we were lucky in having several successive fine days, days which, at that season, we have come almost to regard as normal, the days of relative stillness when in the high air the prevailing strong north-west wind is checked at the onset of the south-west monsoon.

146

In one matter we were wholly in the hands of fortune, and wholly fortunate. When we started, we could not be sure whether the form of the mountain was such that it could be climbed at all. Either there was a way up it, or there was not. As it turned out, there was; and we followed it, more and more captivated. It was easier to follow than we had expected, and, considering the reputation of Kangchenjunga, surprisingly secure. When snow conditions are favourable, there are only two places where risk is unavoidable: the first, under the ice-cliffs on the way to Camp 1; the second, below Camp 2, at the top of the Lower Icefall. The route, complex and full of variety, winds like a thread among difficulties and dangers from which it is itself largely free.

When every mountain over 26,000 feet has been climbed, there will still be in the Himalayas a host of big mountains whose easiest faces and ridges are likely to prove more difficult than the ways first found up the biggest of all; and perhaps the most thoroughly enjoyable sport will always be offered by those whose tops are below the level at which lack of oxygen becomes a burden. Yet it should never be thought that to climb high on one of the biggest mountains is mainly drudgery. The magnificence of such a giant at close quarters is indescribable, and where the stress of wind, sun and frost is enhanced by the rarity of the air, the climber knows that he is at the boundary of the living world.

Twice more, from Rungneet, we saw the untrodden peak: once, in the fading light, indigo and dark red, and again, silvered by sunrise. It had lost nothing of its power to wake desire, though the invitation was no longer individual. Now the mountain seemed to embody the spell of all far places, of all the high snows and hidden valleys that are waiting.

EQUIPMENT

CLOTHING

DURING the walk to and from the mountain most of us wore shorts, a thin shirt, gym-shoes, and a sun-hat. All carried umbrellas.

In the Yalung Valley and above Base Camp, we wore clothing as follows:

Under-garments. Rayon cellular string vest, one or sometimes two wool shirts, and long, loose woollen underpants.

Insulating Layer. Wool sweaters and eiderdown jacket and trousers. The eiderdown suit was made roomy and bulky, and the jacket, which had a hood, came down as far as the lower part of the thigh. The suit gave all the warmth needed, but the design could have been improved by shortening the jacket and having eiderdown pockets on the outside of it for the hands.

Windproof Suit. This was made of the nylon-cotton cloth *Wyncol*, lined with pure nylon. It was large enough to fit loosely over the eiderdown suit, and was in two pieces: trousers, and a simple pull-over smock with a hood.

Gloves. Each climber had one pair of double-thickness silk gloves with fingers, two pairs of fingerless woollen mitts, and a pair of *Ventile* fabric over-mitts. It was most unusual for all these gloves to be needed together.

Socks. A variety of long and short wool socks was taken, and each climber had one pair of eiderdown socks for use in camp. It was unusual to wear more than three pairs of wool socks at a time.

BOOTS

Each member of the expedition had two pairs of boots, a strong rubber-soled climbing-boot of ordinary pattern intended for use as far as 22,000 feet, and a special boot, designed to give protection against cold, for use above 22,000 feet. This special boot, designed for us by the British Boot, Shoe and Allied Trades Research Association, Kettering, and made for us by Dolcis, Ltd., was like the Bradley boot made for the 1953 Everest expedition; the design, however, had been modified in the light of experience both on Everest and, in 1954, on the New Zealand Barun expedition, and the boot was now more compact. Even at the highest camps, it was possible, wearing this boot, to use only one pair of socks and yet have warm feet.

As in the case of the earlier Bradley boot, the sole was of felt and microcellular rubber, and the upper was padded with four layers of *Tropal* (*kapok*); the *Tropal* was protected from sweat, in the Kangchenjunga boot, by a lining of thin rubber; it was protected from outside moisture in part by the thin leather of the boot, but chiefly by a separate over-boot of stout canvas which fitted loosely and came up as far as the knee.

It was possible to make both kinds of boot with the same size of sole, and a climber could wear the same pair of crampons on his two kinds of boot.

These modified Bradley boots were neat enough and tough enough to be worn continually above Base Camp, instead of, as first intended, only above 22,000 feet.

BEDDING

Each member of the party had one air-mattress, a full-length *Lilo* of simple pattern, and two down sleeping-bags. The larger, outer bag weighed about $4\frac{1}{2}$ lb., and the smaller, inner bag $3\frac{1}{4}$ lb.; the inner bag had a zip-fastener along one side and across the foot, and could be opened up as a quilt. This combination allowed a great deal of adjustment to suit temperatures which varied from the heat of a tropical valley to the cold of a high camp.

TENTS

The standard tent of the expedition was the two-man Meade tent made of *Wyncol*. It was 7 ft. long, 5 ft. wide, 4 ft. 6 in. high, and weighed $12\frac{3}{4}$ lb. The design was simplified as much as possible: the tent had one stout guy-rope at each end, and a 12-in. triangular eave along each side with one stout guy-rope in the middle of it; there were only four guy-ropes in all. (See Plate 10.) The sewn-in ground-sheet was of a light, proofed cotton cloth; each tent had two sleeve entrances; there were no ventilators. The poles were of aluminium tubing, in three sections.

Some larger tents of a similar design, the 'large Meades', were taken, but were unsuccessful. They were 8 ft. long, 7 ft. wide, 6 ft. 3 in. high, and weighed $26\frac{1}{2}$ lb. Experience suggests that Meade tents made of a light cloth should not be made taller than 4 ft. 6 in.

For use at Base Camp and below, two large dome-shaped tents were taken, and for kitchen use a number of tarpaulins, measuring 16 ft. × 8 ft. These could be set on aluminium poles as awnings.

MISCELLANEOUS

Climbing Equipment

1. *Rucksacks.* Two kinds were used, a climber's rucksack and a frame pack.

The climbing rucksack, made for the expedition by Messrs. Brown & Best, was a stout and capacious rucksack, without a frame, of conventional continental pattern. It had vertical side-pockets, leather shoulder-straps and a large lid.

The frame pack, made by Beven Napper, New Zealand, was of strong canvas and was shaped like a long sack. It was mounted on a tubular steel frame that was almost flat. There was no pocket and no lid. Extras such as tents could be tied on the frame above the sack.

2. *Rope.* Nylon was used for climbing. There were two sizes, $\frac{5}{16}$ in. diameter (approximately 1 in. circumference) and $\frac{3}{8}$-in. diameter (approximately $1\frac{3}{16}$ in. circumference). Three-quarter-weight Italian hemp ($1\frac{1}{4}$ in. circumference) was used as fixed rope.

3. *Ice-pitons.* Fixed ropes were anchored at the top to angle-stakes of duralumin 3 ft. long. Below, the ropes were tied at intervals to ice-pitons. The pitons were of the 'channel' shape, and 10 in. long.

4. *Crampons.* The Grivel type of light crampon was used, made with the front pair of claws pointing vertically downwards, not forwards.

5. *Ladders.* Light rope ladders made of $\frac{1}{2}$-in. diameter Manila rope, with ash rungs $1\frac{1}{8}$ in. × $\frac{11}{16}$ in. × $7\frac{1}{2}$ in., were taken for steep pitches on rock and ice, and aluminium ladders six feet long, three of which could be bolted together to make an 18-ft. span, for bridging crevasses.

KITCHEN

1. *Cooking-stoves.* Above base, kerosene stoves were used throughout, and solid priming fuel. The stoves were silent-burner Primus stoves with large jets; the nest of pots was enclosed in a heat-retaining aluminium sleeve, as in the standard 'Cooke's Cooker'.

At Base we used a two-burner range, also of the pressure-stove type.

2. *Cooking-pots.*Pressure-cookers were used at all camps up to 22,000 feet. They economise fuel, and make it possible to cook rice, yak-meat and fresh vegetables.

RADIO SETS

Compact and tough radio-telephones weighing 7 lb. each, with battery, were used between camps, and a battery radio-receiver was kept at Base.

FOOD

George Band

In planning the food for the expedition we tried to keep the balance between simplicity, which easily may lead to boredom, and luxurious variety. Above all, remembering one Himalayan climber's advice on food, "the main thing is that there should be some", we planned to take plenty. Although the expedition was to be away from Darjeeling for only about three months, enough European food to last for four months, so we thought, was taken; and it was all eaten.

In general, the Sherpas ate the food of the country, supplemented with small amounts of such imported foods as sugar, jam, and dried milk; and the Europeans ate imported food, supplemented with such foods of the country as potatoes, rice, and fresh meat. Above 20,000 feet the Europeans lived almost entirely on imported food, and the proportion of imported food in the Sherpa diet was increased.

Some highly nutritious foods are unpalatable at high altitudes, and for Kangchenjunga the food was chosen by first asking the experienced members of the expedition what they fancied, and then submitting the proposed diet to Dr. Griffith Pugh, who passed it as compatible, on medical grounds, with health.

The imported food was packed in its original tins or cartons, and some of the cartons holding perishable foods were further sealed in plastic bags. Vacuum packing was not used. The cartons and tins were then packed in weather-proof fibre-board boxes. Food bought locally was packed in plastic bags and sacks.

I. European Low-altitude Ration

Ninety-eight boxes, each containing food for nine men for one day, and each weighing 50 lb. gross.

Contents of Boxes:

BREAKFAST			Sun.	Mon.	Tues.	Wed.	Thu.	Fri.	Sat.
Bacon	.	. .	1-lb. tin		3		3		3	
Sausage	.	. .	1-lb. tin	3				3		
Sausage in beans		.	8-oz. tin			6				6

152

BREAKFAST—*cont.*			Sun.	Mon.	Tues.	Wed.	Thu.	Fri.	Sat.
Porridge oats	.	. 1½-lb. pkt	1		1		1		
Cornflakes	.	. 12-oz. pkt.		2					
Shredded wheat	.	. 14-oz. pkt				1			
Rice Krispies	.	. 5½-oz. pkt.						2	
Weetabix	.	. 9-oz. pkt.							2
Sweet biscuits									
Digestive	. .	. 8-oz. pkt.	1		1		1		1
Regal assortment	.	. 8-oz. pkt.	1		1		1		1
Ginger nut	.	. 8-oz. pkt.		1		1		1	
Ovaltine	. .	. 8-oz. pkt.		1		1		1	
Plain biscuits									
Vitawheat	.	. 14-oz. tin	1	1	1	1	1	1	1
MacVita	. .	. 8-oz. pkt.	2		2		2		2
Ryvita	. .	. 8-oz. pkt.		1		1		1	
Oatmeal	. .	. 12-oz. tin	1	1	1	1	1	1	1
ON THE MARCH									
Dairylea cheese	.	. 3½-oz. carton	3		3		3		3
Sardines	. .	. 6-oz. tin		2		2		2	
Seedless raisins	.	. 12-oz. pkt.	1			1			1
Dates	. .	. 8-oz. pkt.		2			2		
Apricots	. .	. 1-lb. tin			1			1	
Dairy milk chocolate		2-oz. bar	9			9		9	
Fruit and nut chocolate		2-oz. bar		9					9
Nut milk chocolate	.	2-oz. bar			9				
Plain chocolate	.	2-oz. bar					9		
Barley-sugar	.	. 4-oz. pkt.	1	1	1	1	1	1	1
Treacle toffee	.	. 4-oz. pkt.	1	1	1	1	1	1	1
Kendal mint cake	.	8-oz. bar	1	1	1	1	1	1	1
Butter	. .	. 1-lb. tin	1	1	1	1	1	1	1
Fruit cake	.	. 25-oz. tin	1	1	1	1	1	1	1
Sugar	. .	. 5-lb. tin	1	1	1	1	1	1	1
Salties	. .	. 4-oz. pkt.	1	1	1	1	1	1	1
Jam									
Marmalade	.	. 1-lb. tin	1			1			
Strawberry jam	.	. 1-lb. tin		1			1		
Honey	.	. 1-lb. tin			1			1	
Raspberry jam	.	. 1-lb. tin				1			
Blackcurrant jam	.	. 1-lb. tin							1
Drinks									
Orange crystals	.	. 2-oz. pkt.	5	5	5	4	4	4	4
Lemon crystals	.	. 2-oz. pkt.	4	4	4	5	5	5	5
Dried milk	.	. 1-lb. tin	3	3	3	3	3	3	3

On The March Drinks—*cont.*			Sun.	Mon.	Tues.	Wed.	Thu.	Fri.	Sat.
Nescafé . . .	4-oz. tin		1		1			1	
Drinking chocolate	8-oz. tin			1		1			
Ovaltine . . .	8-oz. tin						1		1
Knorr-Swiss soups									
Tomato . .	2½-oz. pkt.		3			3			
Chicken noodle .	2½-oz. pkt.			3					
Asparagus . .	2½-oz. pkt.					3		3	
Mushroom .	2½-oz. pkt.						3		
Egg scramble .	2½-oz. pkt.								3
DINNER									
Stewed steak .	1-lb. tin		4			4			
Corned beef .	12-oz. tin			5					
Tunny fish .	6½-oz. tin				12				
Steak and kidney									
pudding .	1-lb. tin					4			4
Salmon . .	1-lb. tin						4		
Vegetables									
Vegetable macedoine .	1-lb. tin		2						
Peas . . .	29-oz. tin			1				1	
Carrots . .	1-lb. tin				2		2		
Runner beans .	1-lb. tin					2			
Baked beans .	1-lb. tin								2
Fruits and Puddings									
Fruit salad or damsons	1½-lb. tin		2						
Blackcurrants or plums	1-lb. tin			3					
Pears or pineapple .	1½-lb. tin					2			
Peaches or apricots .	1½-lb. tin								2
Christmas pudding .	1-lb. tin		3						
Date or mixed fruit or									
sultana pudding .	11-oz. tin					3			
Chocolate or ginger or									
treacle pudding .	11-oz. tin							3	

2. EUROPEAN HIGH-ALTITUDE RATION

Thirty boxes, each weighing 37 lb. gross. The food in each box was for two men for five days. Each item was packed in bulk, because we did not wish a man to be confronted each day with a "one-man-day pack" containing minute amounts of several foods, some of which he might not like. In practice, at high altitudes, a man confronted with such a pack eats a little, too little, of those foods he can stomach, and throws the rest away.

Contents of Boxes :		*Average Man-day Ration*
1 × 12-oz. pkt.	Quaker oats	1¼ oz.
2 × 1-lb. tin	Dried milk	3¼ oz.
3 × 2-lb. tin	Sugar	10 oz.
1 × 14-oz. tin	Vitawheat	
2 × 8-oz. pkt.	MacVita	7 oz.
4 × 8-oz. pkt.	Sweet biscuits (digestive, assorted, ginger, Ovaltine)	
2 × 1-lb. tin	Butter	3¼ oz.
1 × 1-lb. tin	Jam (marmalade, honey, strawberry, blackcurrant)	1¾ oz.
1 × 8-oz. tin	Drink, (Nescafé, 4 oz., Ovaltine, drinking chocolate)	¾ oz.
9 × 2-oz. pkt.	Lemon/orange crystals	2 oz.
9 × 2-oz. bar	Chocolate (dairy milk, fruit and nut, plain)	2 oz.
2 × 2-oz. pkt.	Glucose	
2 × 8-oz. bar	Kendal mint cake	3¼ oz.
1 × 4-oz. pkt.	Barley-sugar	
1 × 4-oz. pkt.	Treacle toffee	
1 × 12-oz. pkt.	Raisins	1¼ oz.
2 × 3½-oz. pkt.	Dairylea cheese	¾ oz.
2 × 6-oz. tin	Sardines	1 oz.
1 × 10-oz. tin	Rich fruit cake	1 oz.
1 × 4-oz. pkt.	Salties	¼ oz.
5 × 2½-oz. pkt.	Soup (mushroom, tomato, chicken noodle, asparagus, egg scramble)	1¼ oz.
4 × 2½-oz. bar	Dehydrated meat	
1 × 12-oz. tin	Lambs' tongues	4 oz.
1 × 8-oz. tin	Salmon	
1 × 20-oz. tin	Dried egg	1 oz.
3	Fibrecloths (for washing-up)	
1	Tin opener	45 oz.
1 pkt.	Toilet paper	
From supplemen-	Tea	½ oz.
tary boxes	Mashed potato powder	¾ oz.
	TOTAL	46¼ oz.

3. SHERPAS' LOW-ALTITUDE SUPPLEMENT

Fourteen boxes, each to last twenty-six Sherpas for a week. Each box weighed 34 lb. gross, and was intended as a supplement to the Sherpas' normal food, which was bought locally, and consisted of rice, *tsampa* (ground roast barley), *atta* (wholemeal flour), *ghee* (clarified butter), potatoes, lentils, chillies and tea.

Contents of Box:		*Average Man-day Ration*
9 × 2-lb. pkt.	Sugar	1½ oz.
2 × 1-lb. tin	Strawberry jam ⎫	⅓ oz.
2 × 1-lb. tin	Raspberry jam ⎭	
4 × 1-lb. tin	Dried milk	⅓ oz.

4. Sherpas' High-altitude Ration

Tsampa or rice, tea and thirty boxes, each for sixteen men for one day. Each weighed 28 lb. gross.

Contents of Box:		*Average Man-day Ration*
24 × 2½-oz. bar	Dehydrated meat	3¾ oz.
4 × 2-lb. pkt.	Sugar	8 oz.
8 × 6-oz. box	Army biscuits	3 oz.
2 × 1-lb. tin	Butter	2 oz.
2 × 1-lb. tin	Jam (strawberry, raspberry, blackcurrant)	2 oz.
8 × 2-oz. pkt.	Lemon/orange crystals	1 oz.
2 × 1-lb. tin	Dried milk	2 oz.
1 × 4-oz. pkt.	Salties	¼ oz.
4	Fibrecloths (for washing up) ⎫	
1	Tin opener ⎭	
From general	Tea	½ oz.
store	*Tsampa*	20 oz.

TOTAL 42½ oz.

5. Supplementary Boxes

Nine boxes, average gross weight 55 lb., containing food chosen by the climbers to supplement both low- and high-altitude rations from time to time.

Total Contents:	
Brandy	4 × ½ bottles
Rum	2 bottles
Coffee	6 × 4-oz. tin
Golden plums	4 × 20-oz. tin
Damsons	2 × 20-oz. tin
Blackcurrants	3 × 16-oz. tin
Apricots	3 × 16-oz. tin
Peaches	3 × 16-oz. tin

Total Contents—cont.

Pears	3 × 16-oz. tin
Pineapple	2 × 30-oz. tin
Peanut butter	6 × 1-lb. tin
Nut pemmican	6 × 1-lb. tin
Black treacle	4 × 1-lb. tin
Cheddar cheese	2 × 10 lb.
Bounty bars	1 × 3-lb. pkt.
Mars bars	1 × 3-lb. pkt.
Condensed milk	72 tubes
Mixed nuts	6 × 8-oz. tin
Cashew nuts	6 × 8-oz. tin
Shreddies cereal	20 × 8-oz. pkt.
Scone mix	10 × 2-lb. pkt.
Pudding mix	10 × 2-lb. pkt.
Bread mix	10 × 2-lb. pkt.
Potato strip	1 × 12-lb. tin
Mashed potato powder	10 × 8-oz. tin
Dried onion	1 × 4-lb. tin
Dried egg	8 × 20-oz. tin
Custard powder	4 × 12-oz. tin
Baking powder	10 × 8-oz. tin
Margarine	3 × 2-lb. tin
Mustard	12 tubes
Salt	12 × 1½-lb. tin
Dried yeast	5 × 1-lb. tin
Dried apples	5 × 1-lb. tin
Curry powder	1 × 1-lb. tin
Herbs and spices	29 × 1-oz. carton
(sage, mint, mixed herbs, thyme, cinnamon, ginger, nutmeg, mixed spice, paprika, black and white pepper)	
Pickled onions	2 bottles
Mango chutney	4 bottles
Sun chutney	4 bottles
Worcester sauce	1 bottle
Tomato ketchup	4 bottles
Chocolate wholemeal biscuits	2 × 4½-lb. tin
Assorted cream biscuits	2 × 4½-lb. tin
Shortbread biscuits	2 × 4½-lb. tin
Rich fruit cakes	15 tin

6. LOCAL PURCHASE

Summary of food bought locally:

Darjeeling (on departure)

Tsampa, brought from Sola Khumbu	20 maunds [1]
Rice, *atta*, potatoes	9 md.
Dahl (lentils)	3 md.
Ghee (clarified butter)	2 md.
Salt, chillies, curry powder, eggs	3 md.
Darjeeling tea	120 lb.
Fresh vegetables	

Chyangthapu (fourth day from Darjeeling)

Rice, ordered in advance	20 md.

Yamphodin (seventh day from Darjeeling)

Rice, ordered in advance	60 md.

Ghunsa (during the climb)

Rice	11 md.
Tsampa	12 md.
Atta	17 md.
Potatoes	8 md.
Turnips, dried vegetables, eggs	1 md.
Yak	1

After our return, a number of changes which we think would improve the different rations were suggested:

EUROPEAN LOW-ALTITUDE RATION

Increase the soup ration by one-third; double the allowance of lemon and orange crystals; take chicken or ham instead of tunny; vary the cake and sweets as much as possible; add tinned kippers for breakfast; and take a greater variety of tinned fruit: orange, grapefruit, gooseberry.

Below 20,000 feet our luxurious type of ration is advisable if the party is large and if some of its members are not used to Asiatic food; but it is not a necessity, and it is costly, and most small parties will prefer to eat mainly the food that can be bought locally. But above 20,000 feet it is not easy to live on the food of the country: appetizing and concentrated food must be brought from a distance.

[1] One maund equals 80 lb. approximately.

Suggested High-altitude Rations

European	ozs.	*Sherpa*	ozs.
Oats cereal	1	Dried milk	2
Dried milk	2	Sugar	6
Sugar	6	Biscuits	3
Plain biscuits	3½	Meat bar	2½
Sweet biscuits	3	Butter	2
Butter	1	Chocolate	1¾
Jam	½	Lemon crystals	1
Cheese	1	Salt	¼
Sardines	1	Tea	½
Dried fruit	¾	Rice	4
Chocolate	1¾	*Tsampa*	10
Sweets	1¼		32 ozs.
Pure lemon/orange crystals	1		
Tea	½		
Drinks	½		
Soup	1¼		
Meat/fish/egg	4		
Dried vegetables	1		
Fruit cake	1		
Tinned fruit	1		
	32 ozs.		

APPENDIX C

OXYGEN

THE types of oxygen apparatus used on Kangchenjunga were similar in general design to those used on the 1953 Everest expedition, and described elsewhere; but since 1953, thanks to the research done by Messrs. Normalair, Ltd., Yeovil, by the Chesterfield Tube

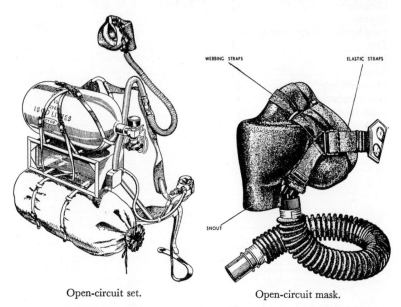

Open-circuit set.   Open-circuit mask.

Company, Ltd., Chesterfield, and by The British Oxygen Company, Ltd., London, important advances had been made in the details of design, and the 1955 oxygen sets were lighter and more convenient to use.

Three types of set were taken: (1) the open-circuit, to be relied on for the routine high climbing of the expedition; (2) the sleeping-set, for use in high camps at night; and (3) the closed-circuit, for

160

trial under particular conditions which were agreed before the expedition started.

A record was kept of the use and performance of the oxygen apparatus, and the technical data obtained by its trial on the mountain should, it is hoped, be of value in advancing the design of oxygen apparatus, not only for climbers, but for others.

THE OPEN-CIRCUIT SET

The main points in the design of this set were (1) a strong and neat carrying frame, well balanced for difficult climbing; (2) a built-in flow-selector with which the climber could without taking

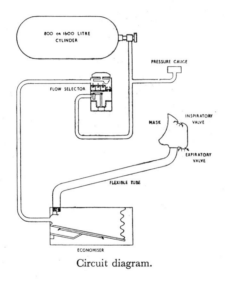

Circuit diagram.

off the set choose one of five rates of oxygen-flow; and (3) a pressure-gauge which was fixed to the frame and was always within the range of sight of the wearer of the set. With mask and tubing, but without a cylinder, each open-circuit set weighed 7 lb.

THE SLEEPING SET

One end of a length of rubber tubing was plugged into the low-pressure side of the reducing-valve of an open-circuit or closed-circuit set. The other end was divided into two or three at a metal junction, and the oxygen carried to the face-masks of two or three climbers. The face-masks were of rubber, and each had a thin rubber re-breathing-bag. The masks covered the nose and mouth, and were kept in place by elastic head-bands. Tubing and two masks weighed 10 oz.

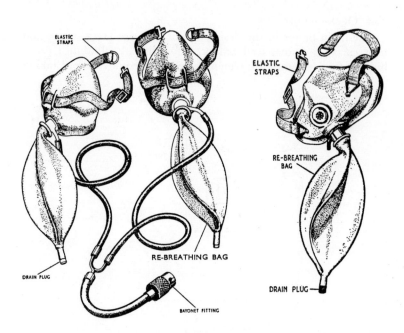

THE CLOSED-CIRCUIT SET

The 1953 closed-circuit set could be put out of action by the freezing of the water in the circuit and by the jamming of the valves by the ice so formed.

Our improved set, which had been evolved from the previous set by T. D. Bourdillon, working in collaboration with Messrs. Normalair, Ltd., had all-rubber valves which could be squeezed to free them from ice, and a re-breathing-bag which was fixed to the soda-lime canister. To put on a new canister was to put on a new re-breathing-bag. The renewal of the bag removed any condensed water-vapour which had collected in the re-breathing-bag while the set was in use, and which was liable, if the set was cooled, for example during a halt in a wind, to freeze.

The set, with mask, tubing, and one canister, but without a cylinder, weighed 19¼ lb. One soda-lime canister weighed 12 lb. and would last approximately as long as a small (800-litre) oxygen cylinder.

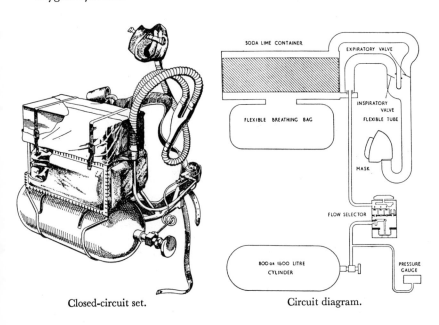

Closed-circuit set.

Circuit diagram.

OXYGEN CYLINDERS

The cylinders used on Kangchenjunga were made of steel, and were wire-wound. There were two sizes: KJ 1, capacity 1,600 litres, weighing 11 lb. 3 oz. empty and 16 lb. charged, and KJ 2, capacity 800 litres, weighing 6 lb. 3 oz. empty and 9 lb. charged. These cylinders had a safe working pressure of 3,750 lb. per sq. in. and their capacity/weight ratios were greater than that of any cylinder used before for climbing: 143 and 129 for the KJ 1 and KJ 2 cylinders respectively, as against 101 for the cylinders available in 1953. The cylinders were brightly painted, the KJ 1 mustard yellow, and the KJ 2 marine blue, colours chosen because they stand out clearly, and because they absorb relatively little heat by radiation. To avoid mental arithmetic while using the apparatus, printed

163

cards, coloured yellow and blue, were carried with the appropriate cylinders: from tables on these it was possible, after reading the cylinder pressure, to find at once for how long the gas in a particular cylinder would last at a chosen flow-rate.

TABLES OF QUANTITIES AND WEIGHTS OF OXYGEN EQUIPMENT

Cylinders:

Number	Type	Capacity (litres)	Total Capacity (litres)
28	KJ 1	1,600	44,800
31	KJ 2	800	24,800
59			69,600

Weights of Sets

Open-circuit with KJ 1 cylinder	23 lb.
Open-circuit with KJ 2 cylinder	16 lb.
Closed-circuit with KJ 1 cylinder	$35\frac{1}{4}$ lb.
Closed-circuit with KJ 2 cylinder	$28\frac{1}{4}$ lb.

Numbers of Sets taken

Open-circuit	12
Sleeping	12
Open-circuit mask assemblies	15
Closed-circuit	2

THE OXYGEN APPARATUS IN USE

On the mountain the open-circuit oxygen set was used by Europeans above Camp 3 (21,800 feet), and above Camp 5 (25,300 feet) by everyone. The closed-circuit set was used by two only of the party, and on only two occasions: during the first exploration of the Great Shelf, when the set was used on two successive days, and on May 23rd and 24th, when Hardie climbed with it to Camp 4, and part way to Camp 5. Sleeping-sets were used, when there was enough oxygen, at Camps 4, 5, and 6.

The general results of the use of these different oxygen sets are here summarised:

THE OPEN-CIRCUIT SET

This set, when used with the KJ 2 (small) cylinder was light enough to be no burden. It was easily operated by climbers with no special knowledge of its use, and it was tough. Sherpas were able to use it at the first trial with very little instruction. With it, at 25,000 feet, Europeans whose gross loads were about 40 lb. were able to climb for several hours at an average speed, including halts, of 300 to 350 feet per hour. As the accompanying table, an analysis of questions later put to the party, shows, higher rates of climbing than this were possible below 24,000 feet. These are not the fastest possible rates, because they are the rates of climbers escorting laden Sherpas who were not using oxygen.

We thought this type of set convenient and pleasant to use, and it gave us all the oxygen we needed. The usual rate of flow used was 2–3 litres per minute, but the high rates, 5–6 litres per minute, were used occasionally, when some exceptional effort was made.

THE SLEEPING SETS

It was usual for two climbers to share a KJ 1 (800 litre) cylinder mounted on an open-circuit frame, the flow selector of which was set to 2 litres per minute. Thus each climber received about 1 litre of oxygen per minute for about six hours.

The effects were wholly good: sleep, warmth, and, on waking, a feeling of well-being.

Occasionally a closed-circuit set was used instead; on these the lowest possible flow rate was 1 litre per minute, shared between two, and we found that this was enough.

THE CLOSED-CIRCUIT SET

Under the conditions of trial these sets worked well and gave no mechanical trouble. The rate of climbing while using this set was little faster than with the open-circuit set, partly because the closed-circuit was tested either on the Great Shelf, where the slope was gentle, or on the Upper Icefall, while escorting Sherpas who were not using oxygen. Those who used these sets complained of heat and moisture, which were, however, bearable. A more serious objection, though a less tangible one, was that when using this set they felt to an unpleasant degree dependent on the apparatus and cut off from companionship and from their surroundings; moreover, the encumbrance of weight and bulk seemed disproportionate to the benefit obtained, and each preferred to use the open-circuit, though knowing that with it his performance, measured in rate of climbing, was poorer.

CLIMBING PERFORMANCES WITH OXYGEN SETS

Chart compiled from information recorded mainly at Base. Weights carried are approximate.

Rates of climb to and from the Summit are to approximate scale only.

Open-circuit sets were used except where shown otherwise.

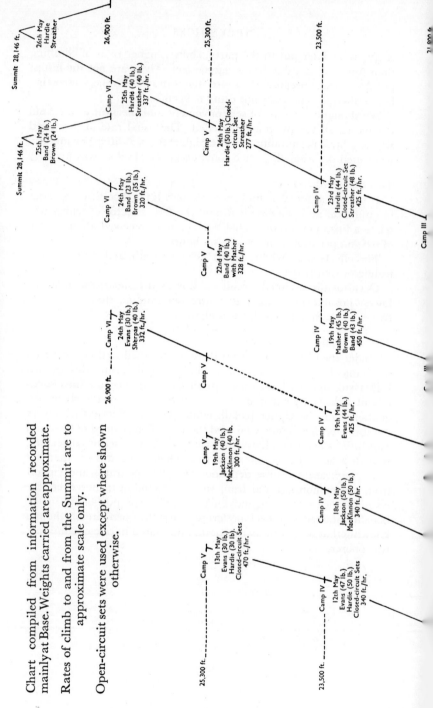

MEDICAL CARE

John Clegg

Preventive Medicine and Hygiene

1. All European members of the expedition were given a general medical examination and were immunized against smallpox, the enteric group of fevers, cholera and typhus. In fact, no cases of these diseases were seen during the expedition, although typhus was said to be prevalent in eastern Nepal at the time.

2. As a prophylaxis against malaria, Paludrine, 100 mg. per day, was given to Europeans and Sherpas. Only one Sherpa had a fever which might have been malarial. No mosquitoes were seen during the expedition, perhaps because the route to and from the mountain was for the most part at more than 8,000 feet above sea-level.

3. The expedition was lucky to have a base camp cook, Thondup, who kept his kitchen clean. At higher camps, meals were prepared by Sherpas with little idea of hygiene, whom it was not practicable to supervise, but even so there were no cases of gastro-intestinal disease directly traceable to infected food.

4. Water-sterilizing tablets were used on the way to the mountain, and were of particular use when passing through the inhabited valleys. From Yalung Camp onwards they were not used.

5. There were vitamin tablets for all members of the party, some of whom took them conscientiously. Those who did not do so remained fit, and the only signs noted which may have been due to vitamin deficiency were occasional bleeding gums.

6. The siting of latrines is difficult where space is restricted, as, for instance, at high camps, and when a large party is following a narrow track in mountain country. At Yalung Camp and above, the frozen, stony ground made digging impossible, and latrine areas were marked off at a distance from the camps. They were strictly used by both Europeans and Sherpas.

7. The only animal parasites met were lice and fleas. Against these 'Gamexane' was used, and, as far as possible, everyone kept to his own clothing and sleeping-bags, though at high camps this

167

could not always be done. Four body-lice were included in one of the summit parties, their vitality at high altitudes and on their return to Base being, according to their host, unimpaired; the party which went to Ghunsa from Yalung Camp collected a quota of lice and fleas; and after a night in a yak-herd's hut on the return journey most Europeans found that they had fleas.

Flies and leeches were so rarely seen as to be no nuisance at all.

ILLNESS

Serious illness was not frequent, but minor ailments were common and there were always a few members of the expedition off sick.

1. *Coolies.*—There were more than three hundred coolies on the outward journey, and sixty on the return. Many of those engaged in Darjeeling were of poor physique and unused to carrying loads; they were ill-equipped for the weather on the Singalila ridge, and here many either deserted or were paid off. The Sherpa coolies, most of whom had come from Sola Khumbu, were made of sterner stuff, and were better clothed; most of these, while ferrying loads up the Yalung glacier, reached heights of 17–18,000 feet, and some of them, on the early carries, showed great hardihood when working through blizzards on the glacier.

Generally speaking, these people were healthy: they suffered as a matter of course from colds, headaches, sore feet, and suppurating sores, probably due to lice, on the face and scalp, but among them there was only one serious illness: at Moraine Camp, on April 11th, one of the Sherpanis had a miscarriage. She refused treatment and, accompanied by her husband, sought the lower valleys.

The Ghunsa people, among whom goitre is common, all wished to take advantage of the presence on the expedition of a doctor, and a part of the duty of Mingma Tenzing, my personal Sherpa, was to deal with those who, having once received attention, joined the back of the queue for a second consultation. During the return journey there was an outbreak, among the Ghunsa coolies, of ophthalmia, which spread to the Sherpas; it responded readily to sulphacetamide ointment, but recurrence was common.

2. *Sherpas.*—In this group there were two cases of serious illness: one of broncho-pneumonia, and one of cerebral thrombosis.

Lobsang injured a rib in a slight fall, and a few days later developed signs of pneumonia. He responded well to injections of penicillin, but his temperature remained high until he had also been given quinine. His recovery was slow, and his illness deprived the expedition of the help of a man of great energy and originality.

Pemi Dorje, who had been very exhausted after the first carry to Camp 5, reached Base Camp on May 24th in a peculiar mental state and complaining of headache. Next morning he was unconscious and paralysed down one side. His coma deepened, and he died thirty hours later. From the symptoms and signs it seems likely that he died of a cerebral thrombosis. About the same time, another Sherpa, Da Tsering, complained of pain in the left calf, where he was thought to have a thrombosis of the veins. He recovered after a few days' rest.

3. *Europeans.*—There were no serious illnesses among the European members of the expedition. Minor ailments included a sprained ankle, two cases of snow-blindness, coughs, sore throats, and thrombosed external piles. Of this there were three cases, and two of them had a previous history of the same complaint.

Dysentery occurred on the journey to the mountain, but was never severe. It responded in a greater or lesser degree to sulphonamides and to streptomycin.

One person was mildly frost-bitten. There was swelling and blistering of all his fingers, and the blisters lasted for about ten days. Other members of the expedition had patches of transient numbness on the fingers and toes; in one case this numbness was followed by tingling and other abnormal sensations which lasted for about three weeks.

EFFECTS OF ALTITUDE

The first weeks in the Yalung were so planned that all members of the party could acclimatize themselves as quickly and fully as possible, and minor upsets due to anoxia were dealt with then and later as they arose.

Yalung Camp was at a height of about 13,500 feet. It was on grass, and space was not restricted. From it various expeditions were made, to gradually increasing heights, until, two weeks after arrival, all European members of the party had reached 17,000 feet, and some had reached 20,000 feet. Thereafter the carriage of stores up the glacier, and the establishment of Base Camp, kept the party constantly at or above 17,000 feet, and no excursions primarily intended for acclimatization, apart from the attempt on Talung Peak, were made.

It is known (Pugh & Ward, 1953) that for acclimatization an adequate fluid intake is necessary. At high altitudes the increased rate and depth of respiration and the low humidity greatly increase the water loss in expired air. Further, temperatures in sunlight may be very high, with much consequent sweating. We aimed at a minimum fluid intake of six pints a day, and many members of the party drank more. The use of orangeade and lemonade crystals made it easier to drink large amounts of fluid, but despite this, urinary output was in general small, and it sometimes happened that for as long as twenty-four hours nothing was passed.

Anoxic men sleep badly; without sleep, they become tired, acclimatize poorly, and deteriorate quickly. At high camps, and in bad weather, when much more than half the day may be spent in the sleeping-bag, lack of sleep becomes serious. Several kinds of hypnotic drug were used. Barbiturates had varying effects: there was much individual difference in the response to them, and some noticed that the drugs were slow to act, and prolonged and un-pleasant in their after-effect. Chloral hydrate was better: it was unpleasant to take, but seemed to have almost no ill results. Many members of the expedition preferred, when once acclimatized, to do without any drug at all.

Loss of appetite was common while acclimatizing, and when above Base Camp. In most cases the appetite later to some extent returned, but no European above Yalung Camp ate as much as on the approach, and all lost weight. One member of the party lost his appetite almost completely above Yalung Camp, but remained fit.

Minor, but nevertheless troublesome, complaints included headache, nausea and vomiting, and sore throat. The first res-ponded well to aspirin, phenacetin and caffeine tablets. For the second, little could be done, but relief could always be got by going down to Base. Sore throats proved troublesome, and no really satisfactory treatment was found. They were probably due partly to injury to the mucous membrane of the throat as a result of cooling and dehydration, and partly to infection. Various throat lozenges and tablets were tried, and pastilles of Gee's linctus were found the most satisfactory. Unfortunately they were regarded by the Sherpas and coolies as a ration of sweets, and the supply ran out long before the highest camps were occupied.

CONCLUSIONS

Generally speaking, the health of the expedition was very good. The journeys to and from the mountain were short, and there was comparatively little opportunity for contact with the local popu-lation. Acclimatization seemed easy, partly because height was gained gradually, and partly because there was ample opportunity for visits to Base Camp and below.

Of particular medical interest was the high incidence of thrombosis. Monge (1942) has pointed out that at high altitudes there can occur symptoms of cerebral vascular disturbance which resolve quickly on descending to lower levels. Men living at high altitudes are polycythæmic (i.e., they have an increased number of red cells circulating in the blood), and on a mountain expedition they are often also dehydrated and for long periods sedentary. The blood is unusually viscous and sluggish, and the chances of clotting are greatly increased. The way in which dehydration may predispose to clotting has been discussed by Houston (1955), and examination of the earlier literature reveals that vascular disturbances, often severe, and not simply due to transient anoxia, have occurred on previous expeditions. Thus, Bruce (1925) mentions a Gurkha N.C.O. dying of a cerebral thrombosis during the 1924 Everest expedition, Tilman (1948) describes a case of cerebral thrombosis in a Sherpa, Pasang Bhotia, during the 1938 Everest expedition, and Houston (1955) describes thrombosis of the calf veins in a member of the 1953 party on K2. The chance of such a misfortune on any one expedition may not be great, but there is little doubt that thrombosis must now be regarded as a condition to which, at great heights, men are liable. Fortunately, now that it is recognized, it is a condition against which some precaution can be taken.

REFERENCES

BRUCE, J. G. (1925), in *The Fight for Everest* (London: Edward Arnold & Co.), p. 68.

HOUSTON, C. (1955), in *K2. The Savage Mountain*, (London: Collins, Ltd.), p. 183.

MONGE, C. (1943), in 'Life in the Andes, and Chronic Mountain Sickness,' *Science*, **95**, p. 79.

PUGH, L. G. C. and WARD, M. P. (1953), in *The Ascent of Everest* (London: Hodder & Stoughton, Ltd.), p. 275.

TILMAN, H. W. (1943), in *Mount Everest, 1938*, (Cambridge University Press), p. 93.

LIST OF EQUIPMENT

1. MOUNTAINEERING EQUIPMENT

Aluminium ladders, 6 ft.		15
Crampons	Grivel 10-point	9 pairs
Crampons	Simond 10-point	32 pairs
Crampons, spare	Simond 10-point	14 pairs
Duralumin stakes, 3 ft.		20
Frame packs	Beven Napper	24
Glacier cream	Simond, 2-oz. tubes	50
Glacier cream	Skreen, 12-oz. tins	10
Goggles	Lawrie's 'Alpine'	72 pairs
Goggles	Lawrie's 'Everest'	4 pairs
Goggles	Hamblin	16 pairs
Hemp rope, $1\frac{1}{4}$ in. circ.		2,000 feet
Ice-axes	Aschenbrenner	25
Ice-axes	Grivel	9
Ice-pitons	Simond	60
Karabiners	Allain	80
Nylon rope, $\frac{5}{16}$ in. diam.		700 feet
Nylon rope, $\frac{3}{8}$ in. diam.		700 feet
Piton-hammers	Simond	6
Rock-pitons	Simond	60
Rope ladders, 25 ft.		4
Route-marking flags		200
Rucksacks	Brown & Best	9
Snow-shovels, American short "T" handle		2

2. CLOTHING

Balaclava helmets	Army	36
Balaclava helmets	Jaeger	9
Boots:		
'Cold Wet' Service		30 pairs
Fur-lined camp		9 pairs
General purpose		9 pairs
High-altitude		25 pairs
Laces		74 pairs
Plastic in-soles		80 pairs

Down Clothing:

Gloves		4 pairs
Jackets	Alpcan	9
	Wico	16
Socks		9 pairs
Trousers	Alpcan	9 pairs
	Wico	16 pairs

Gloves:

Inner wool mitts		37 pairs
Outer wool mitts		37 pairs
Silk, R.A.F. type		25 pairs
Windproof mitts		40 pairs

Pants:

Heavy Service type		40 pairs
Long wool	Army	28 pairs
Long wool	Braemar	9 pairs
Pyjama type		36 pairs

Pullovers:

Heavyweight		9
Heavy cardigan		9
Heavy jerseys, Service type		72
Lightweight		9

Puttees		37 pairs
Shirts	Army	40
Shirts	New Zealand	34

Socks:

H.13	36 pairs
Norwegian	34 pairs
Sea-boot type	36 pairs
Service type	40 pairs
Ski	36 pairs

Vests:

Long wool, Service type	28
Rayon cellular	25
Wool	9

Windproofs:

Braces for trousers	25 pairs
Smocks, Service type	12
Smocks, Wyncol	25
Trousers, Service type	12 pairs
Trousers, Wyncol	25 pairs

3. TENTS

Awnings, 16 ft. × 8 ft. with dural uprights	2
Meade tents, large	4

Meade tents, small	8
Tarpaulin sheets, 12 ft. sq.	6
12-man dome tents	2

4. BEDDING

Lilos, double-layer	9
Lilos, single-layer	30
Sleeping-bags, large	9 pairs
Sleeping-bags, small	16 pairs

5. COOKING

Kerosene	90 galls.
Light aluminium kitchenware was obtained at Darjeeling	
Pressure cookers, Prestige "Commodore"	5
Pressure cookers, Prestige "Minor"	3
Primus, Cooke's cookers	8
Primus double-burner ranges, No. 523/2	2
Primus stoves, No. 54	4
Profol solid fuel, packets of 20 pieces	200 pkts.

6. WIRELESS

Batteries	10
Batteries	12
Hand radio-telephones	4
Radio-receiver	1

7. MEDICAL

Dressings:

Bandages, crêpe	12
Bandages, plain	9 doz. × 4 in.
	9 doz. × 2 in.
	9 doz. × 1 in.
Bandages, triangular	24
Cotton-wool	1 × ½ lb.
Elastoplast strapping	2 × 3 yd.
Elastoplast dressings	1 × doctor's set
Elastoplast	10 × 3 yd.
Gypsona	2 × 2 in.
	14 × 3 in.
	12 × 4 in.
	12 × 6 in.
Gauze	19 × 6 yd.
Jelonet	24 tins

Dressings—*cont.*

Lint	3 × ½ lb.
Safety-pins	4 dozen
Zopla	36 × 1 in.
	2 × 4 in.

Drugs:

Albucid eye ointment	2 × 60-gr. tubes
Aludrox	500 tabs.
Amphetamine	100 × 5 mg.
Anthisan	100 × 100-mg. tabs.
Antivenin	2 ampoules
APC	1,000 tabs.
Aureomycin	376 × 250-mg. caps.
Aureomycin eye ointment	6 × 60-gr. tubes
Aureomycin ointment	3 tubes
Atropine eye ointment	1 × 60-gr. tube
Atropine ointment	2 × 60-gr. tubes
ATS	6 × 1,500 in ampoules
Becosyn	100 ml.
Benzocaine ointment	1 tube
Bradozol	500 lozenges
Cascara sagrada	100 × gr. 1 tabs.
Castor-oil	50 × 15-m. capsules
Chloral hydrate	500 × gr. 10 tabs.
Chloramphenicol	500 × 250-mg. caps.
Chloramphenicol ear-drops	100 ml.
Chloroquin (nivaquine)	100 × 0·25 G tabs.
Cocaine eye ointment	2 × 60-gr. tubes
Cocaine and homatropine eye-drops	110 minims
D.D.T. and pyrethrum spray	4 tins
Dextraven	3 bottles
Dextrose saline 5 per cent	6 litres
Dover's powder	500 × gr. 5
Emetine	48 × gr. 1
Ether	250 ml.
Ethyl chloride	30 ml.
Ethyl chloride	2 × 50 ml.
Gammexane	20 × 1 lb. tins
Gee's linctus	500 tabs.
Gentian-violet jelly	5 × 1¼ oz. tubes
G.G. serum	3 ampoules
Glycerine and blackcurrant pastilles	2½ lbs.

Drugs—*cont.*

Gaunimycin	21 × 4 oz. bottles
Iodine	4 bottles
Kaolin compound powder	250 G.
Mag. sulph and glycerine	6 × 1 oz.
Multivite	1,000 tabs.
Mycil ointment	12 tubes
Mycil powder	12 tins
Nivaquine	500 × 200-mg. tabs.
Nivembin	200 × 350 mg.
Omnopon	10 × gr. $\frac{11}{20}$ ampoules
Omnopon gr. $\frac{1}{3}$, scopalamine gr. $\frac{1}{150}$	8 ampoules
Paludrine	8,000 × 0·1G tabs.
Penicillin (crystalline)	10 × 1 mega.
Pentothal	15 × 0·5G
Pentothal	25 × 1G
Pernicream	6 tubes
Pethidine	50 × 50 mg. tabs.
Phenol ear-drops	1 fl. oz.
Proctocaine in oil	2 × 10 ml.
Proflavine solution tablets	25
Pybuthrin	1 tin
Quinine	200 × gr. 5 tabs.
Rutin	50 tabs.
Skeetofax	36 tubes
Sodium amytal	100 × gr. 1
Sodium amytal	100 × gr. 3
Sodium-chloride solution tablets	25
Sodium seconal	200 × gr. 1$\frac{1}{2}$
Soneryl	200 × gr. 1$\frac{1}{2}$
Sterile water	75 × 5 ml.
Sterile white paraffin	5 × 1 oz.
Sterile yellow paraffin	4 × 2 oz.
Sulphamezethine	1,000 × 0·5G tabs.
Sulphathalidine	1,000 × 0·5G tabs.
Surgical spirit	1,000 ml.

Drugs—*cont.*

Thalazole	200 × 0·5G tabs.
Trilene	500 ml.
Tyrozets	500 tabs.
Ung. meth. sal.	100 G.
Vimagna	2,000 tabs.
Vitamin C	1,000 tabs.
Water-sterilising tablets	25 boxes
Whitfields ointment	100 G.
Xylocaine 2 per cent.	6 × 20 ml.
Xylocaine 2 per cent. dental cartridges	20 × 2 ml.
Xylocaine ointment	3 tubes

Instruments:

Airway	1
Blades (No. 15)	6
Bone-forceps	1 pair
Catheter	2
Dental forceps	2 pairs
Dental syringe	1
Dental syringe needles	2 dozen
Finger-stalls	2 dozen
Forceps, non-toothed	1 pair
Forceps, toothed	1 pair
Giving and taking set for blood	1
Gutta percha	3 pieces
Handle (No. 3) for scalpel	1
Hypodermic needles	21
Kramer wire, 6 in.	2 × 3 ft.
Kramer wire, 4 in.	2 × 3 ft.
Linen thread	1 oz.
Round needles	6
Rubber gloves	4 pairs
Ryles tube	1
Schimmelbusch mask	1
Scissors, blunt	2 pairs
Scissors, sharp	2 pairs
Spencer Wells' forceps	5 pairs
Spud	1
Stethoscope	1
Stretcher, folding type	1
Sutures	1 box

Instruments—*cont.*

Suture needles	9
Syringes	2 × 2 ml.
	1 × 5 ml.
	2 × 10 ml.
	2 × 20 ml.
Thermometers	5
Thomas splint	1
Tourniquet	1

8. MISCELLANEOUS

Altimeters		2
Binoculars	Ross 'Heavy duty'	2
Candles, 9 in. × 1¼ in. diameter		100
Cigarettes		25,000
Hairdressing set		1
Hurricane lamps		6
Prismatic compasses		
Safety matches, boxes		24 dozen
Spring balances		3
Theodolite and survey equipment		
Tobacco		16 lb.
Tool-kit		100
Torches		30
Torch batteries		120
Torch bulbs		100

SUPPLIERS TO THE EXPEDITION

EQUIPMENT AND FOOD

A. EQUIPMENT

1. *Mountaineering Equipment*

Allain, Pierre	Karabiners
Atkinsons	Lipsticks
Brown, Best & Co. Ltd.	Rucksacks
Grivel, G.	Ice-axes and crampons
Kenyon, W., & Sons Ltd.	Rope
Lawrie, Robert, Ltd.	Aschenbrenner ice-axes and miscellaneous
Napper, A. Beven	Sherpa packs
Paul Laboratories	'Skreen'
Ross Ltd.	Binoculars
Simond, C.	Crampons and Crème Mont Blanc, pitons and hammers

2. *Clothing*

Allen, Bastick & Billson Ltd.	Inner and outer wool mitts
Alpcan	Duvet clothing and shoe socks
Bally's Aarau Shoe Co. Ltd.	Boots
Behrmann, H.	Gloves
Braemar Knitwear Ltd.	Pullovers and underclothing
Courtaulds Ltd.	Rayon vests
Dolcis Ltd., and the British Boot, Shoe & Allied Trades Research Assocn.	High-altitude boots
Flint, Howard, Ltd.	Windproof clothing and mitts
Hamblin, T., Ltd.	Snow goggles
Jaeger Co. Ltd.	Socks, cardigans and helmets
Kaiapoi Woollen Co. Ltd.	Shirts
Lillywhites Ltd.	Norwegian socks
Morland Ltd.	Camp boots
War Office	Miscellaneous boots and clothing
Wico, Jean Frey & Co.	Down jackets and down trousers

179

3. *Tentage and Bedding*

Cow, P. B. Ltd.	Air mattresses
Edgington, Benjamin, Ltd.	Tents and miscellaneous items
Ellis, Arthur, Ltd.	Sleeping-bags
Frankenstein & Sons Ltd.	Air mattresses
Ministry of Supply, Didcot	Dome tent
	Stretcher

4. *Kitchen and Cookers*

Black, Thomas, & Sons Ltd.	Miscellaneous items
Burmah-Shell Ltd.	Kerosene
D.E.O.M., Société, France	Butane cookers, reservoirs and spare mantles
I.C.I. Ltd.	Polythene bags
Lever Bros. Ltd.	Soap and 'Surf'
Pepsodent Ltd.	Toothpaste and lipsalve
Platers & Stampers Ltd.	Prestige pressure cookers, whisks, etc.
Price's Candles Ltd.	Candles
Promedico Products Ltd.	Solid fuel
Thermos (1925) Ltd.	Flasks and jars
Westcliffe Engineering Co. Ltd.	Primus stoves

5. *Medical Supplies*

Abbot Laboratories Ltd.
Allen & Hanbury Ltd.
British Drug Houses Ltd.
Cooper McDougall & Robertson Ltd.
Dohm, Sharpe, Ltd.
Eli, Lilly, Ltd.
Flockhart, Duncan, & Co. Ltd.
Hearson, Charles, & Co. Ltd.
Imperial Chemical (Pharmaceuticals) Ltd.
May & Baker Ltd.
Parke Davis, & Co. Ltd.
Roche Products Ltd.
Smith & Nephew Ltd.
Wyeth, John, & Bro. Ltd.

6. *Miscellaneous*

Boosey & Hawkes Ltd.	Tape-recorder
Bowaters Sales Co. Ltd.	Fibre containers
British-American Tobacco Ltd.	Tobacco and cigarettes
Bryant & May Ltd.	Matches
Burgess Battery Co., U.S.A.	Batteries
Craven Pot-hole Club	Rope ladders

Miscellaneous—cont.

Finetta	Camera
Firth Brown Tools Ltd.	Files
Hovenden, R., & Sons Ltd.	Hair-dressing set
Ilford Ltd.	Photographic materials and camera
Imperial Tobacco Company of India Ltd.	Cigarettes
Kodak Ltd.	Photographic materials
Lusk, Andrew, & Co. Ltd.	Packers
Lyte Ladders Ltd.	Light alloy ladders
Minnesota Mining & Manufacturing Co. Ltd.	Recording tape
Pye Telecommunications Ltd.	Radio-receiver
Raytheon Manufacturing Co. Ltd., U.S.A.	Radio-telephones
Reid & Sigrist Ltd	Camera
Remington Rand Ltd.	Typewriter
Rolex Watch Co. Ltd.	Watches
Rolls Razor Ltd.	Dry shavers
Royal Geographical Society	Survey equipment
Smiths English Clocks Ltd.	Travel clocks
Vidor Ltd.	Batteries and torches
Voigtländer, A.G.	Camera

7. *Oxygen apparatus*

British Oxygen Co. Ltd., London
Chesterfield Tube Co. Ltd., Chester-
field   Oxygen cylinders
Normalair Ltd., Yeovil

B. Food

Barker & Dobson Ltd.
Bird, Alfred, Ltd.
Bonded Fibre Fabric Ltd.
Cadbury Bros. Ltd. (Cadbury-Fry Export Department)
Cerebos Ltd.
Chivers & Sons Ltd.
Costa, G., & Co. Ltd.
Heinz, H. J., & Co. Ltd.
Huntley & Palmers Ltd.
Kellogg's Ltd.
Kraft Foods Ltd.
Lusk, Andrew, & Co.
Mann, Palmer, & Co. Ltd.
Mapleton's Nut Food Co. Ltd.

Mars Ltd.
McVitie & Price Ltd.
Ministry of Food
Nestlé Co. Ltd.
Peek Frean & Co. Ltd.
Quaker Oats Ltd.
Quiggin, Daniel, & Son Ltd.
Ready Mixes Ltd.
Ryvita Co. Ltd.
Shredded Wheat Co. Ltd.
Simpkin, A. L., & Co. Ltd.
Smedley's Ltd.
Tate & Lyle Ltd.
Three Cooks Ltd.
Wander, A., Ltd.
The War Office

INDEX

Acclimatization, 30–1, 33–4, 40, 67, 71, 75, 81, 169–70
Aila, 14, 69, 70, 72
Ajeeba, 15, 17
Alpine Club, 9
Alpine Journal, 2, 3
Altitude, effects of, *see* Height
Ang Dawa (of Kunde), 14, 69–72, 97, 100, 119, 138
Ang Dawa (of Namche), 29
Ang Norbu, 91, 94, 103–4, 114, 119, 138
Ang Temba, 29, 91, 94, 96, 103–4
Ang Tharkay, 13
Ang Yangzin, 13
Annullu, 14, 23, 37, 48, 74, 81–2, 84–5, 91, 94, 96, 99, 100, 138
Artificial climbing, ice, 53
Avalanche-s, near first Base Camp, 58; at Camp 5, 105, 107, 110–11, 131; frequency of, 42; on Hump route, 68–9; of ice, 62, 66, 141; of snow, 62–3

Baggage, transport of, 12, 13
Band, G. C., 11, 12; and first Base Camp, 41–3; and Kempe's Buttress, 44–5; and Lower Icefall, 47–8, 50–4; and Hump route, 56, 58–62, 64–5; and summit ridge, 91–2, 111, 114, 117–18, 120–9, 132–3, 138–9; and frost-bite, 120, 126, 133, 169; mentioned, 23, 36–7, 49, 70, 94, 100, 102, 106
Base Camp, first, exploration for, 23, 29–31, 39, 41; occupation of, 41–3; carry to, 47–8, 59, 60; height of, 34; security of, 58–9; abandoned, 55, 59, 60; mentioned, 56
Base Camp, second, occupation of, 55, 58–60; lifts from, 71, 73–4; as rest camp, 75, 77–9, 90, mentioned, 69, 92, 100, 111, 138, 139
Bauer, Dr. Paul, 3, 4
Bauer's spur, 127
Bedding, described, 149; list of, 174; suppliers of, 180
Bell, Peter, 15

Boktoh, 23–4
Boots, 148–9; list of, 172; and rock-climbing, 124; time needed for putting on, 112; suppliers of, 179
Boulder Camp, of Kempe, 26
Bourdillon, T. D., 162
Bradley boot, 148–9
Braham, T. H., 5
Bridge, A. W., 10, 11
Brown, J., 11, 12; and route to Base Camp, 29, 31, 39, 48; and Hump route, 60–2; and Upper Icefall, 66–9, 70–3; and carry to Camp 3, 80; and rock-climbing, 12, 27, 124, 126–7; and snow-blindness, 125, 133, 139; and summit ridge, 91–2, 103–8, 111, 114, 118, 120–8, 132–3, 139; mentioned, 23, 28, 32, 39, 47–8, 81, 90, 94–7, 102
Bruce, J. G., 171

Camp, Base, *see* Base Camp
Camp 1, establishment of, 58, 60–2; described, 60–1, 75; carry to, 71, 73–4; mentioned, 63, 68–9, 91, 94, 141
Camp 2, establishment of, 60, 63–5; described, 75–6; carry to, 63, 66, 71, 73–4; isolation of, 68–9; mentioned, 67, 69, 70, 91, 95, 127
Camp 3, exploration for, 66–7, 70–3; establishment of, 73–4; described, 76, 81–2; carry to, 70–1, 73–4, 80–1; mentioned, 91, 94–6, 141
Camp 4, exploration for, 82–5; establishment of, 85; described, 85, 101–3, 140–1; carry to, 90–1, 139; mentioned, 119, 131–2, 138–40
Camp 5, exploration for, 87–9; carry to, 90–1, 94–100, 130, 142, 169; second carry to, 138; establishment of, 99, 100, 102–8; described, 88–9, 106–12; avalanche near, 105, 107, 110–11, 131; mentioned, 119, 130–1, 138–40
Camp 6, establishment of, 114–18; mentioned, 90–2, 110, 120–2, 128–9, 132–3, 136–8, 140

183